FORGIVING MY
DAUGHTER'S KILLER

FORGIVING MY DAUGHTER'S KILLER

A True Story of Loss, Faith, and Unexpected Grace

KATE GROSMAIRE

with NANCY FRENCH

NELSON
BOOKS

An Imprint of Thomas Nelson

Published in Nashville, Tennessee, by Nelson Books, an imprint of Thomas Nelson. Nelson Books and Thomas Nelson are registered trademarks of HarperCollins Christian Publishing, Inc.

Thomas Nelson titles may be purchased in bulk for educational, business, fund-raising, or sales promotional use. For information, please e-mail SpecialMarkets@ThomasNelson.com.

In rare instances, a name has been changed to protect the privacy of the person described. Events and conversations have been constructed from the author's memory.

Unless otherwise credited, photos are courtesy of the Grosmaire family.

Scriptures are taken from the HOLY BIBLE: NEW INTERNATIONAL VERSION®. © 1973, 1978, 1984, 2011 by Biblica, Inc.® Used by permission of Zondervan. All rights reserved worldwide. www.zondervan.com. The "NIV" and "New International Version" are trademarks registered in the United States Patent and Trademark Office by Biblica, Inc.™

Library of Congress Cataloging-in-Publication Data

Names: Grosmaire, Kate, 1958-author.
Title: Forgiving my daughter's killer: a true story of loss, faith, and unexpected grace / Kate Grosmaire, with Nancy French.
Description: Nashville, Tennessee: Nelson Books, [2016]
Identifiers: LCCN 2015032672 | ISBN 9780718041519
Subjects: LCSH: Grosmaire, Kate, 1958-| Parents of murder victims—United States. | Forgiveness—Religious aspects—Christianity. | Restorative justice—Religious aspects—Christianity. | Christian life.
Classification: LCC HV6529 .G76 2016 | DDC 362.88—dc23 LC record available at http://lccn.loc.gov/2015032672

Printed in the United States of America
16 17 18 19 20 RRD 6 5 4 3 2 1

For Ann

CHAPTER 1

"Andy, can you get the door, please?" I yelled from our upstairs bedroom.

I listened for my husband.

No response.

The doorbell rang, as it tends to do, just as I'd gotten undressed. I kicked my dirt-covered clothes away from my feet and reached for a sundress from my closet.

It was late March. Andy and I had been gardening, as we worked to transform a pasture—where our horse BJ used to live—into a haven for tomatoes, peppers, and beans. We'd inherited the horse years ago from Andy's sister, and when Andy and I worried we didn't have the time to devote to BJ's care, we had found him a nice home in Georgia where they cared for older horses. BJ would be happy in the company of other horses, but it still bothered Ann, our youngest daughter, to see him go. Her boyfriend, Conor, had come over the afternoon BJ left and comforted Ann in the backyard by the orange trees.

Ann had always loved animals. When she was four, she tried to surprise us with a wriggling snake nearly as long as she was tall—and would've succeeded had it not slipped away. Over the years, she carried her guinea pigs—Alvin, Snuggles, Holly, Elvis, Snickers, and Pumpkin—on pillows and wheeled them around the house in a toy school bus. By the time we got BJ, she was twelve. She immediately began caring for him—feeding him, brushing him, and making appointments for the farrier to trim his hooves. Once, while waiting for the vet to arrive, Ann went out to the pasture to sit with her colicky half-ton baby. Though I was intimidated by the animal's size and strength, Ann tenderly stroked his head when he was sick and firmly reined him in when he was healthy.

That little girl in braids was now in college.

After BJ's departure, we had a sunny pasture and a nice pile of horse manure—two ingredients for a great garden. We borrowed a tiller and clawed through the hard-baked dirt. Our daughter Sarah helped us form the five rows in which I'd plant my seedlings. Good gardeners plant several seeds in each container, then weed out the weaklings. But I ignore the directions and give each seed its own space, to offer it at least a fighting chance at life.

Of course, that means I sometimes have more plants than I really need. In February I had started four trays of plants: two trays of tomatoes, one of peppers, one of zucchini and watermelon. Four dozen plants? The entire garden would be packed.

But every seed deserved a chance.

Early that spring, my sugar snap peas and pole beans were thriving, but everything else had to wait until the threat of frost had passed. In North Florida that's around the first of April. During the last weekend of March, I began to transfer the seedlings outdoors. If I was lucky, my tomatoes, peppers, and zucchini would come in just as it was getting too hot for the sugar snap peas and pole beans.

The Florida sun had not yet developed its punishing summer rays, but it was still eighty degrees outside. Andy had pushed a wheelbarrow full of dirt from one side of the yard to the other and was tending the flowerbeds as I worked on my tomato seedlings. I'd already planted the melons and squash, but that day I was planting tomatoes and peppers. I planned to put them in salads and—if the harvest proved abundant—take them to work to share with friends.

As I patted the loose dirt around the little plants with my spade, I whispered a few lines I had delivered that morning in church. "Jesus, remember me when you come into your kingdom." It was Passion Sunday, a week before Easter, and I had volunteered to read the Scripture related to "the good thief" for the gospel reading. The warm soil got under my fingernails, and I wiped perspiration from my brow. While I planted the vegetables, Andy planted flowers. I loved how carefully he arranged them in the beds, as if he were tucking them in. He loves irises, but they won't grow in Florida, which lacks a prolonged cold season. He planted some canna lilies in the sunny areas to make our home look warm and inviting.

Not that we have many visitors. Being situated in a rural neighborhood about five miles outside of Tallahassee, we don't get many drop-ins. Trick-or-treaters and religious doorknockers frequently skip our house, which sits far back on a three-acre corner lot in the neighborhood. Plus, we've never gotten around to making a walkway from the drive to the front door. When friends come over, especially for parties, we have everyone park in the "back forty," which is the grass around the workshop. Everyone who knows us comes in through the back door.

"Andy?" I yelled as I yanked the sundress over my head and rushed barefoot out of my room.

The doorbell rang again.

Undoubtedly, it was a stranger . . . probably a freckle-faced Boy Scout trying to unload overpriced popcorn. I wondered if I had enough cash in my purse.

Andy arrived at the door at about the same time I got to the bottom of the stairs.

"Where were you?" I asked.

"Washing up," he said, but I could tell by one look at him that he'd been interrupted. His shirt and pants were covered in dirt, and the hair around his face was still a little wet from his attempt to clean up.

We exchanged quizzical glances before he placed his hand on the door.

We didn't know it, but that was the last second of "normal" we'd ever have. It was as if the doorknob were invisibly connected to our fate, turning our lives upside down.

Two women stood solemnly on our porch. One was dressed in business attire: white blouse, dark skirt, and dress shoes. The other wore a deputy sheriff's uniform. Her brown hair was pulled back in a tight ponytail, revealing a stern face. I looked out and noticed a Leon County Sheriff's car in the driveway. The lights weren't flashing.

"Are you Ann Grosmaire's parents?" the first woman asked.

Andy nodded.

"My name is Gwen Williams. May we come in? We have some news about your daughter Ann."

"What's wrong?" Andy asked. My husband, the big guy who tenderly plants flowers and gives better bear hugs than anyone, suddenly switched from Sunday afternoon mode into business mode.

"We'd like to come in," she repeated calmly.

One second passed, during which I could tell Andy was surveying the situation. Andy told me later that he had the immediate urge to say, "We didn't do anything wrong!" Strange thoughts go through your mind when a cop shows up on your doorstep. Andy stepped aside, and I showed them to our living room and motioned for them to sit on the love seat. Gwen sat, and the deputy sheriff stood behind her. Andy and I sat on the sofa next to our wood-burning stove.

"I'm a victim's advocate from the sheriff's office," Gwen said.

When she said "victim's advocate," I sighed in relief. At least Ann hadn't gotten into trouble. They weren't there to accuse her of wrongdoing.

But her next sentence evaporated any temporary comfort.

"Ann has been shot."

The sentence hung in the air. My mind raced to fill the space around it.

Ann didn't frequent dangerous areas of town. In fact, her life was pretty idyllic. She worked in a baby boutique that sold gifts for newborns. Earlier that week, I'd asked her about a gift for a pregnant friend who was having a baby shower at church.

"Mom, you have to get the Sophie the Giraffe teether," she said. "It is the most adorable thing ever!"

I looked at the giraffe and bit my lip. It was cute, but part of me wondered if I should just play it safe and get something Diana had put on her wish list.

"No, Mom," she said. "You have to get this one. I recommend it to all my customers." Her enthusiasm caused me to relent. I loved how much she enjoyed the boutique. She'd frequently text me photos of the latest sleepers and laboring gowns. And Ann was right; the giraffe ended up being a hit at the shower.

Was the store robbed? Who would rob a baby boutique? It's hardly a great target. Plus, it's Sunday, so the store isn't even open. Where else could she have gotten hurt? By this time, it dawned on me that Ann was not at work. *Wasn't she with Conor today?*

Conor lived in an apartment building filled with other college students from the area. Were they at his apartment with those roommates I knew nothing about? Did his roommates have guns? Was she visiting him when things got rowdy and a gun somehow went off?

To fill the vacuum left by Gwen's words, my imagination quickly painted a picture of what had happened.

There's been an accident, a terrible mistake. Ann's been shot in her stomach, but it isn't serious. She has a small wound. She's going to survive.

"Is she okay?" I asked. "Is Conor with her?"

Conor was practically part of the family, and in fact, he wanted to make it official. Just a few months ago, he'd told Andy that he wanted to marry Ann. If Conor was with her, I knew he would soothe her until we could get to the hospital.

"Conor McBride?" the deputy sheriff asked.

I nodded.

"Conor was the one who shot her," she said. Her tone was matter-of-fact. Professional. No judgment.

I looked at her blankly, trying to process what she had said.

Conor shot Ann.

Gwen began speaking again. She had a compassionate demeanor, as though she cared very much how we were going to receive her information.

"She's at Tallahassee Memorial Hospital, and we are here to make sure you get to the hospital safely," she said slowly. She clearly had practiced dealing with people in shock. She paused to make sure we understood our options. "We can take you, or you can follow us in your car."

"How is she?" Andy asked. I'd worked at a hospital before, so I knew his question was pointless. No one but doctors can discuss a patient's condition. "Where? How?"

"All we can tell you is that she's holding her own."

Holding her own. That was all we would know until we reached the hospital.

"We'll need our own car, so we'll follow you," Andy said, getting up from the sofa. At home, he's the kind of husband who takes care of things around the house. He happily makes dinner—his specialty is fettuccine Alfredo. But he also has another side of him that I rarely see. As a bureau chief for a state agency, he oversees and manages seventy-five employees. He's used to being in charge, and I knew there was no way he'd be driven to the hospital. Not at a time like this. "I'll drive," he said.

We rushed up the stairs to change clothes and grab our things. *Emergency rooms take forever even with minor injuries,* I thought. *I should change into something that might be okay for a long day at the hospital. Khakis and a top.* Andy put on a T-shirt and shorts. As we were changing, I grabbed Andy's hand. "We need to pray." There, in our bedroom, we held hands.

"Jesus, be there with Ann and be there with her doctors and watch over her and take care of her," I said.

Not a second passed before I added, "And be with Conor too."

Amen.

CHAPTER 2

We followed the sheriff's car to the hospital, which was about eight miles from our house. As Andy drove, I grabbed my phone. "Who should we call?"

"Why don't you wait until we know something," Andy said quietly. Ever since I've known him, he's always been a rock during times of crisis. He doesn't pace or become anxious. He can place his emotions to the side, compartmentalize.

I, on the other hand, fret and worry. Once, when our middle daughter, Allyson, broke her arm after getting a pair of Rollerblades for Christmas, Andy was the one who scooped her up and took her to the emergency room. I was beside myself at home—calling my mom and any friends who would pick up the phone—while Andy was as calm as a windless sea.

Andy put on his blinker to turn onto Miccosukee Road. Even without taking his natural serenity into account, I understood his hesitance to tell people. Putting the situation into words would make it real in a way.

Ann has been shot.

We received the information as we would a stack of mail. Passively. To call someone, the information would need to pass through our ears, hearts, and brains, and then emerge from our mouths. Somehow along the way, it would transform an idea into a fact.

Ann has been shot.

Andy just wanted to focus on driving, on learning the facts, on getting to his daughter. He held onto the steering wheel in the ten and two o'clock positions. Even as I chattered, he didn't speak unless necessary. He didn't speculate.

I searched through the contacts on my phone.

"Who are you calling?"

Even though we lacked information, I wanted to share the news so people could start praying for Ann. I felt anxious, as if someone was squeezing my heart.

"We need to call a priest."

Andy nodded.

I called the church rectory and left a message. Then I called Sherry, a friend of ours who is a nurse in the emergency room.

After that conversation, Andy saw that I still had my phone out. "Just how many people are you going to call?"

"We need prayers," I said. Andy definitely wanted people's prayers, but it hadn't occurred to him that telling people was the first step of that process.

Next I called my oldest daughter, Sarah, who lived in Pensacola, and broke the news. She and her husband, Scott, would drive over right away. Then I called Allyson, a senior at the University of Central Florida in Orlando.

"Do you have anyone who can drive you here?" I asked. I knew she'd be too upset to drive.

"Jamie's here," she said.

"Hand the phone over," I said. I gave Jamie very specific instruction to drive safely and to get Allyson here as quickly as possible.

Then I called Kathleen, a friend from church, and asked her

to send out an e-mail so people could start praying. I provided the only information I had. Lastly, I called Janis, a friend who is an absolute anchor. She's the type of person who's completely willing to be there for someone when needed and willing to disappear when she's not. Everyone's reaction, obviously, was total surprise. But even as I told my dear friends, people all over the sleepy little town of Tallahassee were logging on to their computers and reading about the young man who had shot his girlfriend.

Thankfully, I didn't realize in that moment that our personal tragedy was about to become a public item of interest. I just wanted to get to Ann.

Upon our arrival, a nurse told us a doctor would be in to see us shortly. She ushered us into a windowless room before disappearing into the hospital corridor. We could hear the bustle and noise of the ER outside the door. Doctors being paged, stretchers being wheeled down the hallway.

As we waited, Father Chris from our church showed up, his blue eyes full of concern. Soon after, our friend Sherry showed up, as well as Kathleen.

It's probably just a small wound, not a life-threatening injury, I thought to myself. I knew we wouldn't see Ann until they were done working on her, and I knew that took time. The length of our wait didn't concern me as much as the reason we were there in the first place.

But Andy was a fish out of water in the hospital. With every passing minute, the small room suffocated any hope he had about Ann. He had expected the hospital you see on TV shows, where the doctor meets you in the hall as soon as you arrive and delivers the news.

"Why do you think it's taking them so long?" he asked, his eyes grave with worry. Suddenly our roles were reversed.

"Everything takes time," I assured him. From my hospital

experience I knew that there's paperwork and a procedure for everything.

"I think they're delaying because they just don't want to break the news to us." His voice drifted off.

I glanced at my phone. Its clock automatically adjusted for daylight savings time, which had occurred that day. It confused me, since the clock in the car hadn't been turned ahead. I tried to glance outside, but the windowless room revealed no clues. Andy felt as if we'd waited for hours, but isn't that how time works? The more time you want, and the more you need time to move forward, the more it seems to stand still.

"They're hiding something," Andy said, sitting motionless in his chair. At work he was used to being the one giving orders, making decisions. I could tell it troubled him to sit and wait for someone else to come and give him information.

"You don't know that," my friend Sherry said comfortingly. "The doctor will come just as soon as he's free. Just wait and see what he says."

My phone's reception flickered in and out, but I still managed to alert people of our whereabouts.

Ann has been shot.

No matter whom I told or how many times I said it, it didn't feel real. The trauma settled over me like a fog—keeping me from feeling the cold, harsh reality of the situation.

When a doctor and a nurse finally came in, they stood in the corner of the room. The nurse held a clipboard.

"Ann was shot through her right eye at close range with a shotgun," the doctor said. "She has been gravely wounded. Her right hand was also injured."

A shotgun in the eye at close range? I knew enough about guns to know shotguns spray pellets from a shell. They aren't precise enough to only hit her eye. As my mind raced, Andy asked to see her.

"Really, it's a miracle that she survived."

"What do you mean?" Andy asked.

"After being shot at this range, it's just amazing she's still alive." He paused and added, "Her condition is grave, but stable."

As the nurse led us—Andy, Sherry, Father Chris, and me— back to a large room to see her, that word stuck in my gut. A *miracle?* How dare he use that word! This was not a miracle. It was a nightmare.

It was about to get worse.

When we got to the room, we stopped near a young woman in a hospital gown on a trauma bed. Her head was bandaged.

Ann?

The right side of her head was completely covered with gauze, with just a sprig of hair shooting out. Only a part of the left side of her face was visible. A tube emerged from her mouth.

Was that Ann's mouth? Her mouth was perfect, with full lips I'd kissed a thousand times. Well, when she was little. Over time—I can't remember exactly when—kisses had become hugs, "Mommy" had become "Mom," and our nightly bedtime routine had become "text me if you're going to be late."

Surely I'd recognize her lips.

I stood at the foot of the stretcher. The patient's feet were covered, so I hesitantly lifted the sheets to look at her feet. I saw her ankles, and it began to sink in.

Her arm was exposed beside her body.

Is that Ann's arm? There was so little to judge from.

"Right orbit trauma," I read aloud from the label on the wristband.

"Until the patient's identity is confirmed, they just label the injury," Sherry said. "The tube coming from her mouth is there to . . ."

I looked back at her left hand and spotted a little freckle on her middle finger.

My mind swirled as Sherry spoke. Life—it suddenly felt—was happening around me. Near me. To me.

It was Ann.

Father Chris began to perform the anointing of the sick. This is simply a series of prayers, usually administered to bring spiritual and physical strength to someone who is close to death. Incorporated into the prayers are petitions for the forgiveness of sins.

We watched as he anointed her forehead and did the sign of the cross on her hand. Normally this is done on both hands, but Ann's other hand was bandaged. It was a very comforting—and challenging—thing to observe.

An orthopedic doctor came into the room.

"Mr. and Mrs. Grosmaire, I'm Dr. Lee," he said. "I've been consulting on what to do for Ann's facial reconstruction. Plus, she will need work done on her hand as well. Her fingers have been damaged."

A plan to reconstruct her face? And then her injured hand? Was it possible? Was she going to survive this? How could she? If she did, what would that look like? A few years ago in Florida—and all across America—the Terri Schiavo case had dominated the news, leaving everyone with ethical questions about people who depended on life support. I couldn't help but ask similar questions about Ann. Would Ann actually survive this enough to have her face rebuilt? Would I sit by her bedside day after day, waiting for some sign?

As the doctor spoke, Andy's shoulders softened. After convincing himself in the waiting room that Ann had died, even this horrible sight filled him with relief.

I, on the other hand, had a growing sense of dread. Life as we knew it was over. Whether or not she survived, everything would be different.

Glancing around the room, I noticed a necklace sitting on a

tray. It had been around Ann's neck the last time I had seen her; it was her favorite, and she wore it frequently. The silver chain had a silver rabbit at the end with a small, round, pink stone tucked in his paws. The necklace was sitting in a specimen cup. It was stained with dried blood. Ann's blood.

"Would you like it?" one of the trauma nurses said quietly, picking up the cup and handing it to me.

Someone stepped forward from a corner of the room. A man with green khakis and a matching polo shirt. The shirt bore a badge, and his belt held a holstered gun. A sheriff's detective. "No," he said. "You can't take that. It's . . ." He paused for just a moment, as if every word caused him pain. "It's *evidence*." His eyes dropped to the floor.

Of course.

My daughter's bunny necklace was now part of a police investigation. Along with Ann's necklace, they would also keep her cell phone as evidence. Notebooks in her car. The champagne glasses filled with sparkling lemonade that Ann and Conor had used on their picnic. Everything was evidence.

"After the investigation, maybe, we'll see if we can get it back for you," he said. I set the cup back on the table, then a young woman came into the room.

"I'm sorry to have to do this," she said, her big brown eyes full of compassion. "But I need some information for admission to the hospital."

"Of course, I understand," I said. We stepped just outside the door to fill out the paperwork.

As Ann fought for her life, I dealt with the details. *Sign here. Initial here. We accept cash, checks, and credit cards. May I get a copy of your insurance card?*

I could tell she was uncomfortable asking me for this information, so I tried to assure her that I understood. These details actually provided a momentary respite. I knew how to locate my insurance card and check into a hospital room. I did not know how to deal with a life-changing accident.

As they prepared to move Ann to the Neuro Intensive Care Unit, I went outside to the parking lot to make a call.

"Mom?" I said into the phone. I imagined she was making her evening meal in Memphis. "There's been an accident. Ann's been shot, and you need to come right away. Call Dan or Tim and see if they can drive you." I knew she was too old to make the ten-hour trip alone, but one of my brothers would be able to bring her safely.

Afterward, Sherry offered to take us upstairs to show us where they had taken Ann. We walked through the emergency room, down long halls, up an elevator, and around the corner. The Neuro Intensive Care waiting room had three recliners, some plastic chairs, and a little kitchen. There was also a small desk and a computer. The room only had three walls, and it opened to the hall.

By evening a crowd of friends, church members, and coworkers spilled out from the small waiting area and into the hallway. My friend Jennifer came up to me, put her arm around my shoulders, and said, "There's an article online about what happened. About how Conor turned himself in."

"What do you mean?"

"Apparently, Conor walked into the police station and confessed to killing Ann," she said. "He thought she was dead."

"Where did you read this?" I gasped. What I was thinking was, *Why are you telling me this?* I definitely didn't want to know, but now the information was right there dangling in front of my face. I had to open my eyes and face the situation.

"The *Tallahassee Democrat*," she said. "Apparently, he drove around awhile before turning himself in."

Up to this point I figured something had gone terribly wrong.

An accident. Jennifer's information made the shooting sound more . . . intentional.

The computer just sat there in the waiting room, holding the answers to questions I hadn't mustered the emotional energy to ask; but I sat down in the plastic chair, reached for the computer mouse, and took a breath.

CHAPTER 3

His mother expected him to become a priest, but he couldn't keep his eyes off the girl behind the food counter.

"A chocolate milkshake," he said as he watched her scoop the hard ice cream into the metal canister and fill it up with malted milk.

Even though it probably wasn't the best milkshake he'd ever had, he went to the drugstore every afternoon.

"Another chocolate," he said.

"You must really like milkshakes," said the girl, who was only a high school senior at the time.

Within the year they were married. By the time she was twenty-seven, they had five children—three girls and two boys—of which I was the second. My dad's mother never quite forgave my mom for stealing her son from the priesthood. (My mom didn't buy it. "If he actually had been called to the priesthood," she said much later in life, "he wouldn't have been so easily distracted by the sight of a girl with ice cream.") Even though he never became a priest, my parents loved God and the Church and did everything they could to raise us in the fear and admonition of the Lord. We faithfully attended mass every Sunday. I attended Holy Rosary Catholic

School, made my First Communion in the second grade, and was confirmed in the eighth grade.

This all happened against the backdrop of the exciting but tumultuous city of Memphis, Tennessee. While I was growing up there, a singer named Elvis transformed a Southern colonial mansion into a quirky palace called Graceland, complete with a sheet-music-themed gate of wrought iron, a swimming pool, a racquetball court, and an indoor waterfall. Also in Memphis, the civil rights movement bubbled up as five thousand black Memphians showed up to hear Dr. Martin Luther King Jr. give his first speech in the city. In 1968 he was shot and killed there while standing on the balcony of the Lorraine Motel, and—less than a decade later—Elvis passed away in the upstairs bathroom of Graceland.

Our lives, however, were far removed from the turbulent things going on in the larger culture. My mother stayed home with us while my dad did various jobs, including computerizing the voting system in Memphis. Dad took us to his office, where he showed us how to use a device that precisely punched holes into stiff paper cards. (I knew all about "hanging chads," and how to prevent them, long before the horrible Florida election recount of 2000.) He was a hard worker, but he also had an artistic side; and he made sure to include us in all of his various craft projects, including a rather complicated rooster mosaic from dried beans that we hung on the wall in our den. He also played bridge, did calligraphy, made stained glass, and performed magic tricks well enough to be invited to entertain at parties. My mother tried her best to keep our hectic household of seven in order, as she somehow coordinated all our activities. We always shared our evening meal together as a family, and with five kids, we always had enough players for any card game we could think of.

One Saturday afternoon, when I was fourteen years old, my dad was playing bridge with his friends, and my mom was downstairs.

I was in my room chatting on the phone with a friend. My twelve-year-old brother Dan was somewhere playing with his ten-year-old friend Bart.

"Look what I found," my little brother said, when he found the handgun my father kept in his bedroom closet for personal protection. My dad collected guns, which were arranged quite nicely in a large display case in the living room. Maybe my brother believed that this gun, like one of the antique ones downstairs, was just for show. For whatever reason, he didn't think it was loaded; so he aimed the gun at Bart.

"Freeze!" he yelled.

I was upstairs when I heard the loud bang. My brother had pointed the gun at his friend and pulled the trigger. The bullet went into Bart, who stumbled down the hallway and collapsed.

My mom flew up the stairs and kneeled over Bart.

"Call for help!" she said as she began CPR.

I quickly ended the call with my friend, but after I hung up, for some reason I couldn't get a dial tone. I ran next door, only to learn with horror that the neighbors weren't home. Since I was the one in charge of getting help, I smashed the window to their back door, went in, and called the operator.

I was too nervous to go back into the house. Shortly after the emergency responder arrived, my younger sister came home and my mom asked me to take her for a walk. I was grateful to be away from the frenzied scene surrounding our home. On my walk I tried to make promises to God in return for Bart's life. Bart had been shot through the heart, and nothing could be done to save him.

My father sold all his guns and never played bridge again. A couple of years later, my parents separated for a while. I always figured my dad never got over the guilt of having a loaded gun where someone could find it.

We never really talked about what happened, but it shaped my outlook on life—and on guns and tragedy—forever. My mother particularly avoided the subject. Years after the incident, she was at breakfast with her little group of church friends when someone brought it up.

"Where do you live, Teresa?" one of them asked.

"Kirby Road," she replied.

"Wasn't there a little boy who was shot on that road a long time ago?"

She shrugged. "I don't know about that."

My family kept to ourselves, except when we were surrounded by other like-minded folks at church. Occasionally, when we weren't at church, people reminded us that the South was not typically amenable to Catholicism.

"Catholics are going to hell," a little girl from our neighborhood said at the park.

"My dad says that priests are minions of the devil," said another.

The more people criticized, the more it reaffirmed our differences and our need to stay connected with other Catholic families. In 1972 my family started attending St. Patrick Church in downtown Memphis, which was the first church I'd attended that had embraced the tenets of Vatican II. They encouraged Catholics to have friendships with people from non-Christian faiths, permitted Catholics to pray with other Christian denominations, and suddenly began saying mass in English rather than Latin.

It invigorated me! I loved that the church was willing to operate in the modern world, which was—and is—so desperate for faith. After the 1960s, which had given us the Vietnam War and the assassinations of John F. Kennedy and Martin Luther King Jr., the 1970s were much more relaxed. St. Patrick's mass reflected that spirit. Instead of a traditional choir, we had a bona fide Christian rock band: acoustic guitars, flutes, and tambourines. Our songs had more of a "sing around the campfire" vibe to them than traditional hymns, and the "sign of peace" was a five-minute hug-fest. Once I brought a non-Catholic friend to church, and she was so confused during the "sign of peace" because people walked from one end of the church to the other to get hugs. It seemed to go on forever.

"Is mass over?" she whispered.

The church's charismatic feel connected with my heart.

Then, in 1981, I laid eyes on a tall, blond, and handsome Presbyterian who would also connect with my heart. He was the first man I dated who I felt treated me well. Previously, I'd dated a boy from college who was far too controlling. He would place his hand on my back at parties and guide me in the ways he wanted me to go. Once at a party, I found him making out with another girl—but he insisted that, as my boyfriend, he should take me home. Then, in a climactic end to our terrible relationship, we had a fight outside a pizza place. He angered me so much that I tried to run over him with my moped. It didn't work. First, mopeds aren't that fast, so he had plenty of time to get out of my way. Second, I hit a gravel patch, and the little bike slipped right out from under me.

When I met Andy, I had finally found a man who treated me with sweetness and care. He was charming and attentive, and he always seemed to be laid-back. Two years after we met, we were married in St. Peter's Church.

St. Peter's *Catholic* Church. As one of the oldest structures in Memphis, its vaulted ceilings, hollowed arches, and gorgeous stained glass fixtures made for a stunning backdrop. But the real reason we married in a Catholic church was to make a sacred pact in front of our community. Catholics, like many other Christian communities, don't view marriage as an isolated relationship between a man and woman. Instead, they view it as a partnership that includes future children, the community, the parish, and God. As such, we vowed to raise our children as Catholics.

And we had every intention of doing just that. Once we were married, Andy continued with his college classes, and I continued to work as a records clerk at a local hospital. Though we weren't regular church attendees, we made sure to attend at Easter and Christmas. When God gave us a beautiful baby girl just a year into our marriage, she was baptized at St. Peter's in a private baptism ceremony in the chapel. I was amazed by this little miracle. I would cry thinking about how this person began as just two cells joined together inside of me. I could get lost for hours looking at Sarah's little feet and hands.

After Andy graduated in 1986, we packed all our worldly belongings and drove to St. Petersburg, Florida. There, Andy began a new job as an auditor for a state agency, and Sarah began attending preschool at First United Methodist Church downtown. One day her preschool teacher pulled me aside and invited me to come to church on Sunday. Though I would've preferred a Catholic church, I wasn't sure where Andy—who was still Presbyterian—would feel comfortable.

The Methodist church might be a good compromise, I thought. And for a while, it seemed to be. When we joined the church, I didn't need to renounce any of my Catholic beliefs or be rebaptized, which was a surprise to me after all the insults I'd received in Memphis from people of other Christian faiths. By the time God gave us another daughter in 1988, I was in the handbell choir, we attended church regularly, and Sarah had made little friends. We had our new baby, Allyson, baptized during the church service. I loved the Methodist way of performing baptisms, because it involved the entire congregation. During the ceremony, the congregants renewed their own baptismal vows and promised to help in the raising of Allyson. I loved how connected everyone was, in some small way, to every baby baptized into the church.

But, in the spirit of "covering all bases," I also took her to the chapel at St. Anthony's hospital where I was the childbirth education coordinator and had her baptized into the Catholic Church.

I thought my love for Allyson might just consume me. I was so proud to be the mother of two lovely little girls, and I was overjoyed to discover the following year that I was pregnant again! In fact, our little growing family was preparing for many transitions. By New Year's Eve in 1990, we were on I-75 in a gigantic Ryder truck heading to Tallahassee, where Andy had been transferred for his job.

Our new apartment was just big enough to house our two little girls and the baby on the way. Andy's new position also brought a raise that was big enough to really affect our bottom line each month. Life was full of possibility.

One morning, about seven weeks after we arrived in Tallahassee, I was sitting in our apartment when a horrible thought seized me.

"I haven't felt the baby kick all morning," I told Andy over the phone. Since Andy was at work, I rushed to the doctor's office alone to get checked out—where an ultrasound confirmed my worst fear.

My baby had died.

Unable to reach Andy at work, and knowing no one else in town, I climbed back into my car and sat there for a moment. The sun had warmed the car so that it was terribly hot.

My child had died within me.

I drove home from the doctor's office in a state of shock. As soon as I got home, I called my mother, who flew down from Memphis to help with the girls. The next day I would have to be induced, to labor and deliver my stillborn baby.

"I don't even know where the hospital is," I said to Andy, who had to consult a map to get us there. We hadn't planned on needing the hospital for another three months . . . and not under such circumstances.

My mother stayed home with Sarah and Allyson as we drove away for the procedure. Left alone with nothing but two kids and a heart full of worry, she did the only thing she knew to do. She found our phone book and looked up all the local Catholic churches.

"Hello, my daughter and her husband just moved here," she would explain to anyone who answered the phone. "They don't have a church home, and my daughter just lost her baby. Can you help?"

Some of the church secretaries took notes; others promised to pray. But then a young priest at St. Thomas More, Father Tom Guido, picked up the phone. After listening to my mom's story, he said, "I'll be right there."

He immediately drove all the way across town to Tallahassee Community Hospital, to the bedside of a couple he had never met. Imagine our surprise when a priest showed up—someone we didn't know—during one of the toughest moments of our lives. Though it was a little awkward, I marveled at Father Tom's willingness to drop everything and come to the hospital to help people who didn't even attend a Catholic church . . . all on the insistence of a worried Catholic mama. That's a servant. He prayed with us, offered us what comfort he could, and—two days later—prayed with us again at the funeral of our infant daughter.

"Your sister's spirit isn't in that tiny casket," I said to Sarah, who was six years old at the time. "She's with Jesus in heaven."

Saying that out loud comforted me in a way I had not expected. Until that point, I was focused on her earthly life, her physical connection to me. But really, I had the promise of a life in heaven with her forever.

Her name was Caitlin.

The next time I walked into church, I felt like a stranger. Deep loss sometimes does that. It separates. Because most of the people there had no idea of the loss we had just experienced, there was a part of me they'd never know. A support group called The Compassionate Friends helped me go through my grieving process alongside other parents who had lost children. It put me back on the path to a normal life, and soon thereafter, I saw those two blue lines once again.

"Are you ready to do this again?" I asked Andy.

It was the fifth of March when we casually strolled into the hospital for Ann's birth. She was a week overdue, and a nonstress test just the day before had showed that I was already having minor contractions. The plan was to give me a little medicine—Pitocin—to jump-start things a little. The births of my other children weren't easy—a C-section, followed by a VBAC with an epidural—so I had vowed to do this one as naturally as possible. A midwife, no pain medicine, and a bouncing baby.

It was a noble plan.

"Call Dr. McDavid," I told the midwife as the contractions became too much to bear. "I want an epidural or a C-section, *now*!"

I'd made a big deal out of not wanting either of those for the past few months. But now, I'd had enough.

"Sure," she said calmly. "Let me talk to him and I'll be right back to you."

She returned to the room a few minutes later and just as calmly said, "How about we just give you a shot for pain, and we'll see how you do with that?"

"It won't be enough!" I shouted. I was far beyond caring that my crazy had leaked out.

"Let's just see what this does," she said, injecting the cool, soothing medicine into my arm. "Then we'll decide from there."

It was all I needed. After the medicine took the edge off, I quickly dilated to ten centimeters and pushed out a beautiful, ten-pound baby.

"Look at that!" the midwife exclaimed. "It's a girl!"

For some reason I felt a huge sense of accomplishment over her size and health. I held her immediately and looked at her face. We hadn't decided on a name yet, so I was looking for inspiration.

"Who are you?" I whispered, running my finger over her lips. Sarah and Allyson, whom my mom had brought to see the baby, provided many helpful suggestions.

"We got it," Sarah told me excitedly. "Rainbow Dolphin Star Heart!"

They had come up with a name that included four of their favorite things. Even though the girls had already settled the issue in their minds, inspiration still hadn't struck Andy and me by the time we were leaving the hospital. In the hallway, a clerk stopped us.

"You haven't filled out your birth certificate form yet."

"Yes, I have," I responded.

"But you haven't filled in the name."

"And?"

"You have to give her a name before we can let you take her home."

"Really?" I asked, incredulous. Had National Geographic filmed our interaction, they could've made a thirty-second documentary on what happens when a hospital staffer steps between a mother and her newborn. "You're going to take my baby away from me? Only because I haven't decided on a name?"

I had worked before at a hospital as a birth certificate clerk. On a few occasions I'd let a baby go home without a name, so I knew she was being difficult.

"I'll let you know when we decide," I said as we left with our unnamed bundle of joy.

After we got home, we discussed the main contender for her name: Ann Margaret. Ann because both my middle name and my mother's name is Ann. Margaret because both Andy and I had a grandmother named Margaret.

"Should we worry about people comparing her to *the* Ann-Margret?" Andy asked. We certainly didn't want her to get teased her whole life for having the same name as a sexy starlet who appeared in Elvis flicks.

"No one ever really knows your middle name anyway," I said. "I think it'll be fine." And so, the unnamed baby became Ann Margaret Grosmaire.

∽

Ann Grosmaire, I typed.

I never thought I would be putting her carefully selected name into an Internet search to find an article about her shooting.

When the results came up, I steeled my nerves and forced my eyes to look at the screen.

TEENAGER SHOT IN NORTHERN LEON COUNTY
IN CRITICAL CONDITION AT TMH

A 19-year-old woman is listed in critical condition this evening at Tallahassee Memorial Hospital, the victim of a gunshot wound.

According to the Leon County Sheriff's Office, 19-year-old Conor McBride went to the Tallahassee Police Department at about 2:15 p.m. today and announced that he had killed his girlfriend.

When officers arrived at McBride's parents' house . . . in northern Leon County, they discovered Ann Grosmaire, 19, alive in the house.

Grosmaire had been shot and was unresponsive, according to LCSO. She was taken to TMH.

McBride is being interviewed at the LCSO office.

Conor, I thought, *what were you thinking? Why did you just drive around and leave my daughter all by herself? Was she afraid? Aware at all?*

"Mr. and Mrs. Grosmaire," a nurse said. "You can come back and see Ann now."

We walked back to her room, where Ann was lying in a bed. Her head was still bandaged, and the machines keeping her alive whooshed rhythmically.

"Do you think I can touch her?" Andy asked. He didn't want to hurt or further endanger her. Her condition just seemed so precarious. I could tell Andy was worried that he would make things worse, but how could that be possible?

✑

"Be open to seeing glimpses of God," Father Will said to Andy and me that day at the hospital. "Open your eyes and notice the divine during this trying time. God is with you. Notice it."

Glimpses of God? Well, we definitely saw God in the way our friends and family responded when they heard the news. They kept arriving at the hospital, overflowing from the little area set aside for loved ones as the information ripped through our community like an earthquake. Some people grabbed their purses and their car keys and headed straight to the hospital. Others immediately began praying. Still others began asking around, wondering how to meet any physical needs we had. Even though they couldn't really do much to help, they headed to the hospital with hearts full of sorrow and mouths full of petitions to God.

The hospital staff provided more room for our loved ones, and Andy left Ann's room to thank them for coming. Suddenly he was in the position of comforting the friends who'd shown up from church and work. While he was out in the visitors' area, one of Andy's coworkers—Janet—quietly came up to him and motioned to a man standing near the elevator.

"Who's that?" she whispered. Andy looked at the man. His hair was gray, almost white. Dark eyes. He slouched against the wall as if he wanted it to absorb him.

"Is that Conor's father?" Janet asked. Conor had worked for Andy's office, and Janet knew him. "He looks an awful lot like Conor."

Andy walked through the sea of well wishers, deliberately making his way to the man. He wasn't sure what he would say, but he crossed the room of people with a rare single-mindedness and purpose.

When he finally got to him, the two men looked at each other.

Frequently in times of tragedy, the community blames the parents of the perpetrator. After school shootings, for example, the media and the culture come down hard on the parents.

Why didn't you see this coming?

What did you do so wrong to create such a monster?

Instead, Andy knew that Michael McBride, in many ways, was the only other person in the hospital who could begin to grasp what he was feeling.

They were both fathers who had lost a child. Though Ann was in a hospital room and Conor was somewhere in jail, deep down they both knew they'd irrevocably lost their children.

When Andy's eyes met Michael's, he didn't punch him in the nose or start screaming obscenities. Rather, he reached his arms around him and pulled him into his chest. I've always compared Andy to a big teddy bear, calm and loving. Kind and compassionate.

The hug lasted for a few seconds—seconds packed full of emotion and regret.

"I'm glad you're here," Andy finally said. "But I may hate you by the end of the week."

Michael simply nodded.

"Do you want to see Ann?" Andy asked.

CHAPTER 4

*T*hree weeks before their high school prom, about a year before Ann was shot, she and Conor went out on a date. They had been dating for two years, and there was no doubt that they would attend prom together. I appreciated Conor for many reasons. He had a solid head on his shoulders, he seemed to really care about academics, and Ann was crazy about him. I developed a sweet, nurturing relationship with him . . . one that Andy did not strive to replicate. Andy is sometimes known as "Mister Uh-oh" at work because he's called in when things have gone bad—or, if someone needs to be let go, people always say "Uh-oh!" when they see him. I'm not sure what kind of boy Ann could've brought home that would've pleased Andy . . . and the guys seemed to pick up on that.

I looked through the upstairs window and saw Conor pulling in to drop Ann off. It seemed like only five minutes had passed when I noticed Ann speeding out of the driveway in her car.

"Andy, where's Ann going?" I asked.

"She just got a call from Conor," Andy said. "He's been in an accident."

I couldn't believe what he was saying. I had just seen him with my two eyes in what seemed like seconds ago.

"Let's go see if he needs help," I said.

About a mile from our house, we saw Ann's Volvo pulled over on the side of the road. The ambulance and the police car were already there, lights flashing. Conor's vehicle had rolled over completely and was back on the right side of the road. The front of the car had been smashed down more than the back. The windshield was completely shattered.

Conor was conscious and sitting in the ambulance. His face was covered in tiny cuts, but otherwise he seemed fine.

"The car hit the tree and rolled over," said the sheriff. "You can see the scrapes on the top of the car where it slid down the pavement."

"How could he have survived that?" I asked while looking at the car. "It seems like a miracle."

"Well, the Honda has side air bags as well as front," he said. "It may have been a miracle, but those air bags helped. He must have been going sixty miles per hour."

Ann told us that Conor had seen a deer crossing the road. He went off to the right, then overcorrected and hit the tree.

"I haven't ever seen deer on this road," I said. Though I didn't say it at the time, it seemed sort of suspicious that a deer had caused such a bad wreck. Part of me wondered if he had simply been speeding on the road and gotten careless. Shortly after those thoughts went through my mind, his dad parked behind us and walked up quickly.

"Where's Conor?" he asked, his voice full of concern and emotion.

He would be fine, of course.

‎⁓

I sat next to Ann and watched her in the hospital bed.

Oddly, I didn't feel like I was helping her by being there. I was in the room with her, but I had no sense of her being there, or of her being aware of my presence. She looked asleep, but I didn't feel any of the warm feelings of comfort I used to feel when she was a child who had finally drifted off.

Instead I felt cold.

When Andy came into the room, I looked up and smiled, welcoming the company. He had someone with him. I felt a hint of recognition. *Someone from church? From Andy's work?* I was not familiar with all his coworkers and employees.

The man had slumped shoulders and a frown etched on his face. As he followed Andy into the room, I stood to greet him. The bed was between the door and my chair. When our eyes met, I gradually recognized him.

Michael McBride?

I paused.

Can I go to him?

Without even a second to contemplate what I was doing, my feet answered my own question. I walked around the bed. Even as I approached him, I thought, *Can I embrace him?* That was the word in my mind.

Embrace.

The Holy Spirit is sometimes described as a wind, without shape or form. In that moment this mysterious, unseen force propelled me across the room, around the foot of my unconscious daughter's bed, to the father of the boy who put her there.

Can I embrace him?

Again, my body answered my own question. I don't know what I would've done had I been the one to see Michael as he stood by the elevators. I don't know what it would've been like if Michael had waited until the next day to come to the hospital. But in that moment, in Ann's quiet, semidark hospital room, God's grace moved me across the room, and my arms reached out and hugged him.

Crossing that room, I took the first steps of my journey of forgiveness.

"I'm so sorry," he said. "I haven't been able to talk to Conor yet. We were on vacation, so I drove straight here."

After talking for a few minutes, I left to see who was in the waiting room. I hadn't wanted to sit in Ann's room for a long period of time, but I didn't want her to be alone. Since Andy was there to take a shift, I walked out of Ann's room and into the hallway teeming with people—congregants, friends, family. At the time, Andy had started a five-year program to become a deacon in the Catholic Church. Cindy, the wife of another man in the program, had seen the news online and told her husband, "We have to go to the hospital." My husband knew her husband well, but the wives only got together one day a month for a retreat. Even though we wives weren't terribly close, she did whatever was necessary to take care of the people in our group.

"We just have to be here," she said.

This seemed to be the predominant sentiment for several people. When I walked out into the hall, I was overcome with love. Seeing so many people from my community—probably forty or fifty—felt like being wrapped up in a warm blanket.

They all wanted to help.

I used to teach parenting and breast-feeding classes, and when I counseled young moms-to-be, I'd say: "Keep a list. People are going to ask you what they can do to help, so write everything down that could possibly help you. When someone calls and asks what they can do, you can look at your list and say, 'Thanks—we need toothpaste.'"

I would also tell them that it's as much about friends wanting to help as it is about the moms needing help. People want to do for people in need, and it's kind to let them. After all, in this terrible place Andy and I found ourselves, a tube of toothpaste was not going to salve our wounds.

But the love of a community could.

That advice came back to me as I was surrounded by people who wanted to show me love.

What can I do to help?

Is there anything I can do?

"I don't think the cats have any cat litter," I said, ever practical . . . and still in shock. Amid all the drama, the first thing I remembered was that I hadn't been able to buy cat litter that afternoon for our three cats.

I'm sure people were flummoxed by the request, but everyone received it as if it made all the sense in the world.

Cat litter? Okay.

Several priests were at the hospital to tend to us. Father Chris had stayed the whole evening. Father Will, not even ordained a year, Father Michael, and Father Kevin all came to the hospital to be with us.

As I looked at these men of God, with their clerical collars and kind expressions, it made me thankful to be a part of the Catholic Church.

I had a soft spot for Father Mike, an Irish gentleman with snow-white hair, kind blue eyes, and a compassionate, loving manner.

"Do you want to see Ann?" I asked him. As we walked back to the intensive care unit, he took about five or six steps then stopped.

I followed suit by stopping and waiting with him.

He took five or six more steps before stopping again.

I stopped with him and silently waited. That's when I noticed that his eyes were full of tears.

"Father Mike," I said. "It's okay."

"Kate, it's not okay."

When I looked into his eyes, it felt as though God was speaking to me.

This is not okay with me. This is not what I want. I'm grieving this too. I feel this loss just as greatly as you do.

It wasn't a long moment. It only lasted a second or two. But that's when I strongly felt God sharing in my grief—that he cried with his children, that this was definitely not okay. People sometimes ask if we ever blamed God for this tragedy. We haven't. Perhaps any brewing anger dissipated when I saw the tear-filled eyes of Father Mike, who shared in our sorrow just as he'd rejoiced in our past triumphs.

Hours passed, filled with beeping machines, nurses coming in and out of Ann's room, visitors, and whispered conversations about what exactly happened that had made Conor do this. By 11:00 p.m., I was absolutely exhausted.

I felt a little like I did after I brought Ann into the world so many years ago.

After a successful labor and delivery, the nurses had let her stay with me in my room. She nursed and suckled until I needed a break. Finally, I said, "Is there any way you could take her? I'm so tired."

"Oh," one said. "We thought you would want to keep her in the room." The nurses knew me because I taught breast-feeding classes at the hospital.

"Yes," I said, handing the tightly wrapped bundle to the nurse. "But I just need some rest!"

Nineteen years later, I was in another hospital, during a less joyous time, realizing once again the limitations of my body.

"I want to go home," I said to Andy. We'd been sitting by Ann's side for hours.

I knew there were mothers who would not have left their child's hospital bed under any circumstance. They'd vow to stay right beside their injured child's side, hoping against hope for a miracle. They'd sit stoically in the stiff chair. They'd go without rest on the off chance that their child would wake up and see they'd been there all along.

I needed sleep—real, deep, restorative sleep, not the constantly interrupted hospital sleep. I'd just received the most shocking and horrible news, and I knew the disruption to our lives had only begun.

"That's fine, I understand you want to go home. But first, you stay here while I go home and take a shower, and then I'll come back and spend the night. I want to be here when Ann wakes up," Andy said, kissing my forehead. I looked in his eyes and saw something I didn't possess. Hope.

I nodded, knowing God *could* perform a miracle. It wasn't as though I was overcome with hopelessness, but I couldn't shake the belief that she'd die of her injuries. Part of me loved how Andy still had hope, and part of me was deeply saddened by it.

Andy reached into his pocket for his keys, when his fingers landed on some change. He pulled out the coins and saw that one of them was a gold piece about the size of a quarter. He picked it out from the others on his palm to look at it more closely. On one side was an image of an angel rising out of the clouds.

"Look at that," he said, marveling at the coin.

"How'd that get in there?" I asked.

"Maybe that's what Father Will was talking about when he said, 'Be open to seeing glimpses of God,'" he said.

That little coin convinced us that—somehow—God was very close in that moment.

When we emerged from Ann's room, to our surprise the four priests and our deacon were still there. These men are early risers, so their remaining there touched Andy deeply. We came out and hugged each person. With every hug, Andy thought, *This is why I go to church. This is why I belong to a community.*

Deacon Tom took one look at Andy's weary eyes. "Need a ride?" he asked when he heard of Andy's plan to go home and return.

A hug. A ride. A comforting word.

We never felt more loved and taken care of by our community.

That is, until I got home.

Just a few hours earlier, a deputy sheriff and a victim's advocate had shown up on my porch and shattered our world. That night—at one thirty in the morning—I arrived to that same house, to the place that would never quite be what it had once been.

And on the porch I found cat litter—one hundred pounds of it.

CHAPTER 5

When I got back home, the house seemed like the shell of something that had previously held our happy lives. My muddy gardening clothes lay in a clump on the floor. How different the world looked when I'd slipped those on earlier that day, when my head was filled with plans for my tomato plants.

What I didn't know—what I wasn't told until many weeks later—was what happened at the hospital just as I was falling asleep at home.

Around two o'clock that morning, Andy was still awake in Ann's room. It was dark and quiet, except for the whoosh of the ventilator. The machine almost sounded like it was explaining how it was doing the heavy work of living for Ann. *Innnnn. Ouuuuut. Innnnn. Ouuuuut.* Andy stood over Ann's bed, just looking at her.

"Everything's going to be okay," he said. "I'm here."

He paused and listened to the ventilator, a poor and inadequate substitute for Ann's voice. He didn't really expect her to respond, but he was surprised at how desperate he felt when she didn't.

"If you can move or say anything, go ahead," he encouraged softly.

Innnnn. Ouuuut. The machine whirred.

"It's okay," he added. "I know it probably hurts a lot."

He stood there without saying a word, feeling the desperation of the situation settling on him.

Then, amazingly, he heard something beyond the ambient night-time sounds of the hospital.

Forgive him.

He didn't stop to wonder where this was coming from. He knew. He'd heard the voice for nineteen years. It belonged to the same girl who had only mastered five words—none of which was *Mama*—when she was two years old. It was the same voice that belonged to the girl who called trees "ghees" and cats "gats" when she was three. It belonged to the girl who required speech therapy until she finally conquered the "f" sound. The little girl who one day triumphantly announced, "Daddy, listen: 'The *f*armer chased the *f*ox over the *f*ence!" It belonged to the same girl who would later ask to borrow the car and a few dollars for a soda at the bookstore.

Her lips weren't moving, but he heard that voice just as clearly as he'd heard it when she asked him to make her and Conor dinner for their picnic.

Forgive him.

"No," he said aloud. "I'm not going to do that." How could she ask such a thing? How could she expect him to even consider forgiving the person who changed our lives forever?

Dad, this is what you need to do. You need to forgive.

"He did something terrible, Ann," he said. "I won't forgive him."

Dad, you need to forgive Conor.

"No way."

You need to.

"I won't."

Had someone walked by the room, they would've wondered why Andy was arguing with a comatose person. It was a real discussion—one that any father and daughter would have over more trivial topics and in happier circumstances.

After about twenty minutes, he realized it was a back and forth he couldn't win. Ann would never relent.

"Okay," he said in exasperation. The girls always got what they wanted in the end, and this exchange would be no different.

After all, what father can refuse his daughter?

"I'll try."

CHAPTER 6

$\mathcal{M}$iriam?" I said the next morning, after walking over to my neighbors' home across the street and knocking tentatively on their door. Even though we were friendly, I didn't make it a habit of stopping by unannounced.

"Would you mind keeping an eye on the house for me?" Ann's shooting was headline news in the papers and on television. There weren't many Grosmaires in the country, and we were certainly the only ones in Tallahassee. "Of course," she said. "Do you want Randy to mow the lawn?"

"You know, I just planted all my tomatoes in the garden," I said, shocked at how long ago that peaceful afternoon seemed. "If he could just go over a couple of times this week and turn some water on them, that would be great."

"He'll make sure things are okay, Kate," she said, her voice catching.

Like a powerful magnet, this tragedy drew all our family from across the southeastern United States to Tallahassee Memorial Regional Medical Center. Specifically, to a tiny waiting room with plastic chairs and a coffeepot in the corner.

One by one, they showed up, disheveled and concerned after

making their unexpected trips. My mom had traveled nine hours straight from Memphis with my brothers; Andy's brother came up from St. Petersburg, Florida; his sister drove from Robertsdale, Alabama; and my sister Patti drove up from Davie, Florida. They all had the same shocked look of disbelief and concern on their faces when they saw me for the first time. While we waited for information on Ann, a dozen family members crowded into the small room until one of the deacons at our church—Deacon Melvin, who was also the chaplain at the hospital—offered to let us use a classroom down the hall.

"As long as no one's using this room for a class," he said, "you guys can hang out here."

Everyone fit nicely into the huge boardroom, which had a long table down the middle with plenty of chairs on either side. Notably, the room had large windows that made it roomy and bright. Andy's office staff brought lunch up for us—platters of chicken fingers and little sandwiches—which they did every day we were in the hospital.

It gave us a much more comfortable place to visit with people who'd traveled a long way to see us. Every act of kindness, every visit gave us a taste of God's love. It felt as if God were hugging us over and over and over again, through the arms of our family, our fellow parishioners, our neighbors. I was very aware of their collective anguish, perhaps the result of God spreading out our grief so we wouldn't be crushed under its weight. As our church, family, and community mourned with us, it lightened our burden and saved us from despair's depths.

"I've never experienced a Holy Week like this one," said Father Mike as he stood in the waiting room over the people gathered at the long table. Ann was shot on Palm Sunday, the day on which Christ began his Passion, and it felt as though our friends might've been walking with us toward her eventual death. A small group in the corner held hands, bowing their heads and praying. Another group was gathered around a table, setting out snacks. Cindy was encouraging people to sign up for the online meal volunteer system, which ended up providing two months of amazing casseroles, hams, and pies.

As we fellowshipped with our visitors, we were interrupted by consultations with various specialists. A reconstructive specialist asked to speak to us about Ann's hand, which was injured by the blast of the shotgun. After looking at Ann and consulting his charts, he looked at us earnestly and explained what could be done.

"She needs to be stabilized before we can do any sort of surgery. Because of her brain swelling, her skull is left open," he explained. "Once that is stabilized, here's what I'll do to salvage her hand."

After his presentation, he left and I watched the nurse tinker around Ann's body, tending to her as she appeared to sleep. Caring for Ann used to be my job, but her injuries had far exceeded anything I could solve with Neosporin, a kiss, or some strategically placed Band-Aids. I knew I'd never be able to reach over and grab that hand of my daughter's again, but the visit with the specialist was unnerving. I feared my daughter would not survive the week, so her hand was way down on my list of topics that needed to be addressed. In the hospital everyone had their own area for which they were responsible, which made it hard to get a good overall picture of what was really going on.

But, deep down, I felt I knew.

I went out of the room to get some air and visited with friends near the waiting room, outside the Neuro ICU. That's when our friend Rick Palmer turned the corner and dashed up to me with the confidence of a man used to navigating hospitals.

"I came as soon as I heard," he said. Rick and his wife, Barbara, have two very well-manicured acres in a neighborhood a few miles from our home, with neatly trimmed driveways and well-mulched flowerbeds due to Rick's gardening hobby. In addition to ornamentals, Rick grows the most awesome tomatoes, eggplants, and beans in his backyard. He and I always "dished the dirt," so to speak.

Of course, he wasn't there to talk about eggplants. Rick is also an ophthalmologist, a corneal specialist, and the staff ophthalmologist for three hospitals—including Tallahassee Memorial.

"I can help with her eye," he said. Like everyone else, he simply wanted to do something to make things better. His offer to help with her eye was like a mom's offer to bring over a casserole. But as I listened to him explain his possible services, it seemed so futile.

"I'm not sure, Rick. No one has said anything about removing her eye," I said. "I don't know if or when they might do it."

But Rick was so insistent. He wanted so badly to help us.

"Andy said I could see Ann," he said. "Do you mind?"

"Certainly," I said. I was convinced that tending to her nonfunctioning eye was not the best use of our time at this point, but I figured a nurse could explain it to him better than I could.

"I'm Dr. Palmer, and I'm an ophthalmologist," he said to a nurse. "What can I do to help?"

"Thank you, but . . ." She looked at me and paused. "I'm not sure there's much to do right now."

"I can enucleate the eye, for example, to try to salvage it," he suggested. Enucleating simply means removing the eye from the socket, a practice done after orbital trauma. "If you need me to," he insisted, "I can do that. I've been in medical practice for years, and I could easily help."

She looked at him blankly.

"Please," he said. "I want to do *something*."

Very calmly, and in a measured fashion, she said, "That's not necessary."

"If the eye isn't functional," he said, "it will need to be taken out."

"No," she explained again. "It's not necessary in this case."

"It's a common procedure," he insisted. "I can do it today."

"There's *nothing* to remove."

He was shocked by her answer.

"Nothing?"

"Nothing."

The realization gradually settled on him. He couldn't enucleate the eye because there was no eye. Part of her—a very significant part of her—was simply gone. Stolen.

"You're sure?" He just stood there for a moment, trying to wrap his head around just what *nothing* meant, not wanting to process it.

"Thanks for trying, Rick."

Rick tilted his head as if there were some answer written in the ceiling tiles, and his eyes suddenly filled with tears. He quickly dropped his head, turned to me, and shuffled out of the room, where Andy intercepted him with a big hug in the corridor.

"I'm sorry," Rick said to us, sniffling. He was shaking his head in disbelief. "I just got overwhelmed in there." Rick has three daughters of his own, and a young son.

"Every tear someone else has shed," I said, "is one I don't have to cry."

As Andy comforted Rick, my deepest fears were being confirmed. Ann would not recover. Previously I'd imagined an eye tucked under those bandages somewhere. Now I could only imagine red nothingness where her right eye, her "good" eye, used to be. This is the one she depended on because the other one was considered "lazy," despite being strengthened through exercise over the years.

And that's how I realized that—even if she survived—I'd never look into her beautiful, deep, chocolate-colored eyes, inherited from her Native American grandmother, ever again.

⌒

I understood Rick's despair at not being able to do anything productive to make the situation better. "If there's anything I can do," our friends said at the end of most conversations, "please let me know." People want to "do" for you in a time of crisis, and there was very little that could be done.

As I sat in the hospital, I tried to think of more practical ways for others to help. After all, I didn't need another hundred pounds of cat litter. I didn't know of it at the time, but there's a Jewish tradition of bringing a hardboiled egg to a grieving friend or loved one. It's supposed to symbolize eternal life, but there must be a certain amount of practicality involved as well. Giving a mourning person an egg gives them just the right amount of protein, exactly what they need when food is the last thing on their mind. In a similar vein I tried to accept nourishment from eager friends. Every morning, when the first person offered help, I'd ask them to get me a smoothie from the hospital food court—peaches and cream. I knew I wouldn't eat unless someone put food in my hand, so those daily smoothies—which I'd nurse until lunchtime—helped a great deal. Some days, it was the only nourishment I had.

I visited with friends in the impromptu snack room until we were called to visit with the trauma surgeon. We left the little cocoon of family, love, and sandwiches to meet the cold harsh reality of Ann's prognosis. I wasn't sure how to feel, but I knew I wanted actual information. I didn't want another confusing report, or the narrow view of a specialist. I wanted to know what we were dealing with.

We had to be "buzzed in" to the Neuro Intensive Care Unit. It was a large room with ten smaller rooms surrounding the nurses' station in the center. Ann's room was the first one on the right. The trauma surgeon smiled kindly as we walked up to the nurses' station where she waited to speak to us.

"We've decreased Ann's pain medications," she said to us. "We're hoping to see some sort of response."

"And?" Andy asked. I detected it again, sitting right there below the surface. Hope.

"Nothing yet," she said, "but there's so little we know about the brain, you just never know. We're going to continue evaluating her."

The doctor spoke with the certainty that anything could happen. But Ann, completely unresponsive, didn't seem like she was on the verge of a turnaround.

"With modern medicine," she continued, "there's a lot that can be done."

I wanted to believe, and as she spoke I tried to conjure it. *Miracles happen. The brain is mysterious. People are praying.*

Should I believe? Should I hope?

"We'll have to see," she said. "I'll keep you posted as we continue to monitor her response."

When she left, I felt uneasy and unsettled, unable to wrap my mind around Ann's true condition. I'd hoped the conversation would provide clarity, but I only felt uneasy.

Was it possible that she could survive a blow from a shotgun at almost point-blank range? Though Andy was willing to hope, I didn't feel I could entertain the idea of her survival.

When the neurosurgeon came into the room later that day, the hopeful tone created by the trauma surgeon dissipated.

"Mr. and Mrs. Grosmaire," he said as he walked in, immediately getting down to business. "Has anyone shown you the CAT scan?"

"No," Andy said.

"Would you like to see it?"

"Certainly," Andy said. "Visual things help me understand."

He brought the CAT scan up on a computer monitor. The scan took data from several X-ray images of Ann's head and converted them into pictures. They had taken an X-ray, moved down slightly, taken another X-ray, moved down slightly, and taken another. The resulting CAT scan was composed of probably twenty different images.

"Let's start from here," he said. The screen was blank, just dark, until we saw a little circle of grayish-white in the middle. "That's the top of her skull." Then, the second picture expanded a little bit and we saw a little bit more. At some point, as I was looking at it, I recognized that we were actually seeing Ann's head. It was sort of like looking at a bread loaf, one slice of bread at a time.

"What are these?" I asked. I'd noticed two or three little sparks of light on the image. They weren't just little round dots; they appeared to have little rays coming off of them as well. Almost like stars.

"Every point of light is a shotgun pellet," he said.

I swallowed hard as the CAT scan moved down her head. In one image, there were three or four little pellets, but in the next there were ten, then fifteen, then more.

"There are so many," Andy gasped. "It looks like a night sky."

As the images went down her head, I realized a horrible fact that had been cloaked when the nurses had said to us, "Maybe you ought to step out of the room while we change her bandages."

On the scan, I began to clearly see her left eye socket, the left side of her cheekbone, skull, jaw, and teeth. On the right side there was nothing but blackness. With a deep, horrifying jolt, I understood what the other doctor didn't have the fortitude to tell us.

Not only was Ann's eye missing. The whole side of Ann's brain was gone.

The doctor rolled his finger down the mouse, and the images scrolled more quickly.

As the slides moved from one to the other, the pellets grew in density. The quick motion and appearance of the shiny, starlike pellets made it look like fireworks going off on the screen—which meant, of course, in Ann's head.

"This will show you just how devastating your daughter's injury is," he said in an almost professorial manner. He pointed directly to a place where the pellets went into Ann's head. "Here, you'll see the point of entry. The trauma that the brain has endured is extensive. She has just minimal brain function."

"So." I gathered myself. "You're saying the Ann we know and love has been lost?"

He paused, but only for a moment. The previous doctor seemed more concerned with sparing our feelings, but this one seemed intent on telling us the horrible truth. I scarcely can imagine how two professionals could deliver such different takes, all in the course of one afternoon. As much as I hated what he was saying, I appreciated his straightforwardness.

"She has brain stem function, and that's about all," he said. "She'll continue to deteriorate."

"Her brain," I said, pointing to the CAT scan, barely able to formulate the question. "It should be here, right?"

"Correct," he said. "But that's not the only concern. The pellets going through her head certainly caused devastation. But the shock of the blast also destroyed the tissue in this part of her brain as well."

I grabbed Andy's hand, as the sensation of losing Ann—really losing all hope—made my soul plummet.

He continued, "Her organs will eventually shut down, and her body will continue to deteriorate to the point where even the ventilator won't be able to sustain her." He took his hand from the computer mouse and looked directly at us.

He delivered the various pieces of bad news with the regularity of a metronome, one piece after another, with just enough time between his sentences to make sure we understood.

Afterward, we shuffled though the halls. I couldn't stop thinking about her organs shutting down. Would that mean that she'd eventually have a feeding tube? Would that be something we would want to do?

As I've mentioned, we'd been inundated with details of the famous Terri Schiavo case because she had also lived in Florida. The legal battle was heart-wrenching to watch, as courts eventually were forced to decide whether or not to honor Terri's husband's request to remove her feeding tube or Terri's parents' request to leave it in. Though many doctors and court-appointed physicians diagnosed her as being in a vegetative state, her parents (and the doctors they hired) didn't believe it. Heartbreaking photos and videos of Terri were shown on the news for more than seven years, as they battled over her life. Politicians, churches, and families had heated conversations about the morality of "pulling the plug" on her life, or what was left of her life. The husband was described as greedy and selfish for wanting to move on with his life. The parents were criticized for being unrealistic. Ultimately, the tube was removed.

Our scenario was not like Terri Schiavo's yet. No one was pressuring us to make a decision about a feeding tube. When it was mentioned, it was presented as a future possibility, something to consider in case it came up. But our conversation with the neurosurgeon made it seem like a certainty.

What would we decide? Would we suddenly be embroiled in a complicated moral situation? As we walked through the hall, various tidbits of Church doctrine bounded around in my head. Before this moment, I was sure I knew how the Church viewed such instances. We err on the side of life, but what if there's no hope?

I didn't have time to consider these issues as we walked, our footsteps echoing in the otherwise empty halls. When we got to the waiting room, all eyes went to us. Our family members, who had been chatting quietly at the table and eating from platters full of little sandwiches, froze when they saw the expressions on our faces.

"Things don't look so good," Andy said, standing at the head of the table.

He repeated everything the neurosurgeon had told us. As we spoke, we could see their eyes filling with tears. "But we want you to know that she's not suffering. She never suffered."

My son-in-law Scott openly started crying, and my sister Patti got up and hugged me.

"Does that mean . . . ?" she asked. No one wanted to ask if death was imminent. Though I'd already gotten there in my head, I could see Andy was still torn. It was disorienting to receive such different reports from doctors in such a short amount of time, but the CAT scan didn't lie. Half of Ann's brain was gone; the other half had been injured from the blast.

I cut Patti off before she said the obvious. Ann was going to die, but I didn't want to hear those words spoken. "We know where this road will lead us, but we don't yet know how long it will take to get there."

❧

"Can we talk to you a minute?" I asked Father Chris Tuesday afternoon. He had a beard, which gave him more of an authoritative air than his three years of priesthood would otherwise garner. He followed Andy and me to the classroom we were using as a waiting room and pulled out a chair from the table that still held remnants from lunch—some plastic cups, a paper plate with sandwich crusts, and empty cans of soda.

"How can I help you?" he asked. He had a quiet and wise nature, which made you want to spill your secrets or ask for advice. Because he'd studied in Rome, we considered him a theological scholar.

"So," I began, "we've been told that the Ann we know and love is gone."

His face fell at the news, but he didn't look away or interrupt us with words of comfort. He just listened as we relayed the prognosis from the neurosurgeon.

"We've been told Ann's injuries are grave," I explained. "One by one, her organs will fail, which means that eventually we'll need to make some hard decisions."

"God can work a miracle," Andy said. "But at this point, it would take one to save Ann's life."

"We're not asking what to do," I said. "But it would be helpful to understand what the Church teaches on end-of-life matters."

Because I'd been in church for so many years, I felt I had a pretty good understanding of this subject. But there was something about how suddenly this issue landed right in our laps that made me want to hear directly from a church authority.

Father Chris listened carefully and sympathetically as we spoke. Then, when he was sure that we had finished, he spoke words of comfort and love.

"First, I'm so sorry that you're faced with such a decision," he said. Even though he was young, he had the bearing of someone who'd ministered people through all types of painful situations.

"Second, the Church respects life, but not to the point where they believe you should keep someone alive at all costs."

"What about a feeding tube?" Andy asked. "We're not sure we want to do that, because it seems like it's prolonging the inevitable."

"The Church would not suggest you prolong someone's life just because you medically can," he said. "The Church doesn't require you to keep life going under such a circumstance." He explained that the Church allows people to follow their own consciences, but that it is helpful for our consciences to be informed by the Church's beliefs on such matters. "You're following the right path," he said. "And you would be doing nothing contrary to the teachings of the Church."

Father Chris didn't make the decision for us, but he helped confirm our inclinations about the feeding tube. Though no one was directly asking us the question, we'd settled in our hearts that we didn't want one.

In addition to the daily updates from Ann's doctors, we continued to receive updates from the Leon County Sheriff's detectives, Don and Dawn. Dawn had shared with us on Monday what Conor had revealed in his confession: that he and Ann had gone on a picnic to celebrate her making the dean's list, but somehow they had started arguing. They argued all night until Conor fell asleep, then they continued the argument the next day when they woke up. When Ann left the house, Conor got out his father's shotgun with the intention of killing himself, but Ann knocked on the door and he let her back in. He waved the gun around to frighten her, and when it was pointed at her, he pulled the trigger.

"So, Conor has pled not guilty to attempted murder," Don told us on Tuesday.

Did I hear him correctly? It made no sense to us.

"Had he not already confessed?" I asked. "Why would he plead not guilty?"

"Ma'am, it's just procedural. The defendant has to appear before a judge in a timely fashion. They had to charge him, and he had to plead not guilty. Now his lawyer can start his discovery."

The words rang in my ears. *Attempted* murder? If Ann died, I realized, the "attempted" would be dropped.

"What if Conor didn't want to be charged with murder? Could they do something about that?"

"What do you mean?" Don asked.

"I don't know. On TV, they file an injunction or something to keep the victim alive so that the defendant won't be charged with murder."

"That never happens," Don assured us. "I've never seen anything like that happen in real life. You have the right to make any decision you need to, and they can't stop you."

I should have known better than to believe an episode of a TV crime drama, but how could I have known what to expect? I hated being so ignorant of the legal aspects of what was happening, but I was grateful that the detectives took the time to explain things to us.

That evening I was sitting in Ann's room when the nurse came in to tend to the ventilator.

"Did you know she's breathing on her own at times?" she asked as she looked at the monitor.

"Really?"

"Yes, she's really just on assisted breathing, see?" The nurse extended her finger and pointed at the screen. "This ensures she takes a deep enough breath. But if you watch this number, you can see she sometimes is breathing by herself."

"Wow," I said. "What does that mean?"

"She's a fighter. Sometimes she'll get tired and ride the vent, which means she relies on the ventilator to breathe for her for a while," she said. "But she's fighting."

Ann was a fighter. As devastating as the news concerning her injuries was, here was a little piece of positivity. She was giving us the time we needed to process everything. To allow everyone to see her one last time. My daughter was a fighter.

⁂

"Do you mind if I pray?" our friend Bob Schuchts asked Tuesday evening. Bob was a counselor involved in the healing ministry at church. He and Andy had crossed paths during one of the weekend retreats Andy attended fourteen years earlier. I got to know him through many interactions over the years. We could tell he was in shock at seeing Ann in the hospital bed, but mostly at seeing what we were living through.

The prayers of our community seemed to be lifting us up and protecting us from the depths to which we could've sunk.

"Please do," Andy said, as we all bowed our heads.

"Wait," I said, opening my eyes for a moment. "Will you pray for the McBrides too?"

"Conor's parents?" he asked.

"And Conor," I said, very deliberately. I hadn't had time to really process all my feelings toward Conor or the McBrides. However, I knew our response to them needed to be right and full of grace.

"We're getting so much love and attention from our friends and community, but they've lost a child this week too," I said. "They're not a part of a church body, so I don't know if anyone is reaching out to them."

Tragedies bring out the best and worst in us, and, as mentioned before, often people's attempts to explain a horrifying event turn into accusations against the perpetrator's parents. *What kind of parents would raise a kid like that? They must've done something really wrong. How did his parents not see the types of magazines he read? Didn't they notice he was gloomy? Didn't they see the warning signs?*

To help make sense of it, people have to establish rather quickly that there's a significant difference between the way they've raised their families and the way a murderer was raised. It's a reassuring myth.

This couldn't have happened in my family.

While we were losing our daughter, our community was rallying around us. As the McBrides were losing their son in a real way, they were being isolated from their community. Their lives would forever be marred by what he'd done—isolated by unspoken accusations, unanswered questions, and wild suspicions.

"It's easy to feel sorry for us," Andy continued. "But what they're going through—being the parents of someone who did something terrible—has to be . . . in a way . . ." His voice broke. "Worse."

Bob didn't respond, but I could tell that he was deeply touched by what we were saying. Instead, he simply bowed his head and prayed.

"Lord Jesus," he began. In those two words, so much anguish, compassion, and love. Sometimes when people prayed for me during these times, I didn't necessarily hear all of their careful words. Instead, I just let myself feel swaddled by them, as a baby feels the comfort of a bunting.

A few minutes into the prayer, Bob stopped praying when he heard a knock on the door. I jolted back into reality. Instead of being lifted up in prayer before the throne of God, I opened my eyes and saw that I was just in a hospital room—institutional white tiles beneath my feet, and fluorescent lighting washing the life out of me. Andy dropped my hand, walked across the room, and pulled open the heavy wooden door.

On the other side of it were Michael and Julie McBride.

We'd already seen Michael, who'd come to visit just hours after the shooting, but this was the first time we'd seen them as a couple. Bob stood to leave, but I motioned to the chair in the corner. "Stay. Please."

"We can't say we're sorry enough," Julie blurted out, tears running down her face.

I walked over to Julie and gave her a big hug. I didn't quite understand all that had happened over the past two days, but I knew this: we were bound to the McBrides in a way that no one else could understand, and we needed to be with them during this time.

"Do people come by?" Andy asked the McBrides. Every day their address had been published in the newspapers as the location of the shooting. "Are you getting phone calls?"

"Not really," Michael said. "In fact, it's been quieter than you'd think."

"Is the press hounding you?" I asked. I imagined the media camping out on the doorstep of the McBrides' home, giving them no space to grieve without cameras flashing in their faces.

"Yes, but we aren't answering their questions," Michael said. "No one wants to hear what we think."

"We have people from our church who are praying for us all day. We've asked them to pray for you too."

Julie looked down at the Kleenex Andy had given her. "We had friends who came by the house even before I got home to clean things up." I thought of her coming home to a house surrounded by Do Not Enter tape, and of the women who were caring enough to spare their friend what was inside.

"How is Katy?" I asked. Two years younger than Conor, Katy was his sister with special needs. I remembered a conversation that I'd had with Ann and Conor about the possibility that they might have to care for Katy later in their lives.

"We told her that Conor did something bad to Ann, and that he had to go away to be punished. She doesn't quite understand it all. How can I explain it to her?" Julie replied.

I took Julie's hands, looked in her eyes, and said, "We don't define Conor by that one moment."

There's no way to understand a person's essence by judging one moment of his life. If we defined Conor only as a murderer, that would mean defining my daughter only as a murder victim. If I left him in that place, I was leaving her in that place too. I refused to leave Ann there.

Another memory came to me, of an afternoon talk show with

a mother so distraught over her daughter's murder that years later she still cried daily. She could not get past her daughter's death. The show's counselor asked her if she was honoring her daughter's life by only focusing on the way she died. Ann was an incredible young woman, and I wasn't going to let one dark moment overshadow her life. I had to let go, let go of anything that would hold me in that dark place—which meant forgiving Conor.

"Who would want to be defined for the rest of their life by the worst thing they ever did?" I asked.

No one answered, the silence affirming the truth we all knew. We are more than our sins.

Later, Bob described the moments of stillness and quiet during this initial meeting as "a hush of the presence of God." Even though it was the Holy Week of Easter, perhaps the best soundtrack for the interaction would've been "Silent Night." There was a calmness, a tenderness so powerful it was almost palpable. One could easily imagine heavenly hosts surrounding us and singing alleluia in that moment. It was a night of redemption, of people quaking at the sight of such loss, such love. Both loss and love. Strongly. At once.

But Ann wasn't sleeping in heavenly peace. She was fighting for her life.

Andy cleared his throat and broke the silence. "How's Conor?"

"He's still at the Leon County jail. He's on suicide watch in the medical pod," Michael said.

"You haven't visited him?"

"I've only spoken to him." He noticed my surprised look, and explained, "He's nineteen, so he's not a juvenile. That means they don't give the parents any special visitation. We're trying to get a good defense attorney now, and we're hoping to see him soon. I know he just added Julie and me to the list."

"What list?" Andy asked.

"The jail allows him to make a list of people who can visit

him," Michael said. "He only gets four, and we're two of them. He wants to add you, too, Kate."

"Me?"

He nodded solemnly, looking at the ground. "Now that Conor's named his four, the list can't be changed for a month."

"Why me and not Andy?" I said. It seemed to me that he'd want a man-to-man talk after everything that happened.

"Conor's so sorry about what happened," Michael said, slowing down the words to make them somehow fit the scope of the moment. Normally when someone apologizes, it's over something insignificant. *I'm so sorry I spilled my wine on you. I'm sorry I'm late. I'm sorry I forgot your birthday.* I could tell Michael was struggling over the inadequacy of the words. He was right to struggle, because words weren't enough. His "sorry" couldn't change what happened, heal our devastated hearts, or put Ann back at the Thanksgiving dinner table. But what the McBrides didn't know—what perhaps I didn't even know—was this: I was beginning to forgive the man who shot my daughter.

Conor put me on his visitation list for a specific reason. In a way, it made sense. We'd grown very close over the years that he and Ann had dated. For a couple of months he even slept under our roof. When the police told us that Ann had been shot, my first question was "Where's Conor?" I knew he'd be one of the first people she'd want by her side.

If Sunday hadn't happened, Conor and Ann would've been dreaming about engagement rings. It was hard for me to suddenly recategorize him from *almost family* to *the enemy*.

"It'd help him so much if you could go," Michael said in a slightly pleading tone. "He'd like to see you."

I tried to speak, but I felt a catch in my throat. From the very beginning I cared about what was happening to Conor. Even when I read online that he'd driven around for forty-five minutes before turning himself in to the police, I wasn't outraged. I was gravely disheartened and anguished over his behavior. But I wasn't angry.

That didn't mean I wanted to go down to the jail and see Conor. I just didn't *not* want to see him.

My name had taken up a space on a very short list. It implied an obligation.

Would I be able to meet it?

CHAPTER 7

*I*t seemed I was living in a tragedy I'd seen on television before. When the deputy and the victim's advocate showed up on our porch, I thought, *I've seen this on television.* When the doctor broke the bad news to us, I figured, *I know how this goes.* As I wondered about Ann's death, I braced myself for the dramatic showdown that would inevitably occur with Conor's attorney, thinking, *It's happened a thousand times.*

Perhaps we'd seen too many courtroom drama movies.

About nine months before Ann was shot—on Father's Day—Andy and I were relaxing in the living room when Ann and Allyson came in and lingered near the sofa.

"You need something?" Andy asked. He recognized the look on both their faces. This was going to be a tag team effort.

Allyson smiled an awkward smile and came over to us. "You know how you always taught us to take care of animals? That if we find one that's sick or injured, we should make sure it has shelter and help?"

We looked at each other, then Andy looked over their shoulders, expecting to see (or hear) their latest rescue. "Go on," he said, waiting for them to reveal just what they had found.

The story spilled out. Ann had gotten a call from Conor. He was at a friend's house, having literally been thrown out of his house by his dad. He had nowhere to go and only the clothes on his back.

"Can Conor stay here?" Ann blurted out, bracing for an immediate denial of her request.

"Where is Conor now?" I asked. The girls glanced past the kitchen to the small room off the carport. Conor shuffled in, his head hung low.

A lost puppy would not have looked more forlorn. His eyes were red as if he'd been crying, but there was more—red marks on his face. Fighting with his father? On Father's Day of all days? It occurred to me how little we really knew about the parents and family life of the young man who was dating our daughter.

"What happened, Conor?" I asked him gently.

"I asked for the car to go to the movies," he said. "My dad said no, and we started arguing about it. One thing led to another and all of a sudden, he just picked me up and threw me out the front door."

I knew we were hearing only one side of the story, but the immediate problem was this young man standing in front us with no place to go. Compassion came first. Along with some rules.

Conor and Ann had just graduated from high school, and they were about to really experience the world in college. Conor had been accepted to Stanford but had chosen to go to Tallahassee Community College so he could be closer to Ann. Maybe by opening our home, we could help his last summer before college be less tension-filled.

"Ann," Andy said, in his most serious dad-voice. "He can stay, but he'll have to sleep in the rabbit room." This wasn't a bedroom with a cute rabbit motif; it was more of a mudroom or spare room where we had kept our pet rabbits when we first moved into the house. It had plenty of room for a spare bed and was where we often put visitors.

"Of course," she said, leaning over and hugging me.

"But I'm going to call his mom to make sure she knows where her son is," I said. "I bet she's worried sick."

"Fine!" she gushed.

I called Julie to tell her that Conor was at our house. She shared with us that the family had been in counseling. *That's good news*, I thought with relief. I offered to make sure that Conor showed up to any appointments.

"It's good they are working through their issues," Andy said, relieved, before adding sternly, "and make sure he knows counseling is a condition of him living here."

He lived with us for a couple of months, until he got an apartment with a few other guys while attending Tallahassee Community College. During those two months, we had the chance to get to know Conor. Even though it wasn't ideal—he and his parents should've been enjoying their last few months together before he went to college—we grew close to Conor, and he became a part of the family.

Conor was the type of teenage boy I appreciated. Not the Eddie Haskell type: "Why, Mrs. Grosmaire, you look quite lovely in that outfit." Nor was he a mumbly-mouth teen who wouldn't look you straight in the eye. He said "Yes, ma'am" and "No, ma'am" and even offered to do chores around the house when he stayed with us— like clearing brush and mowing the lawn.

We also had serious conversations about his life at home. I counseled him to work toward making himself the best person he could be and urged him to be accepting of his parents' shortcomings. We can only change ourselves, and we can't expect others to change for us. We are each on our own healing journey. He took it all in as much as any eighteen-year-old could. I know it would have been hard for me at eighteen to think I was the one who needed to change and not my parents.

Once Conor moved into his apartment, he suddenly became less of a family member. He and Ann had begun attending classes at Good Shepherd that would lead to Conor joining the church at Easter. But being across town at school, and with no transportation, he stopped attending the classes. Then, it appeared that Ann and Conor were no longer dating.

One day she stopped by my office and asked to use my phone. Clearly Conor was not answering when he saw her number flash up on the screen. When she called him from my phone, he answered. From the half of the conversation I heard, it seemed she wanted to meet and talk things over, but he was refusing.

On another occasion Andy and Ann were riding through Tallahassee on some sort of errand, when Andy posed a question.

"Does being with Conor make you a better person?" he asked.

They drove silently for about a mile before Ann burst into tears. She never answered.

As with previous breakups, this one lasted only a few weeks. Soon they were back together again, and whatever tension had existed for those few weeks was gone.

That fall, Conor came to Andy and asked for a job. Though Andy wasn't convinced it was a good idea, he thought it might give Conor a chance to prove himself in the workplace—in the mailroom, actually. He took in the mail, sorted it, and passed it out to people at their desks. He also did odds and ends—scanning, moving paper from one desk to another, and anything else that popped up over the course of the day. Andy wasn't his direct supervisor, so he figured that giving Conor a job would offer him the opportunity to make a little money and to better himself.

If working for Andy was an effort to demonstrate maturity, it failed. Right off the bat, Conor showed up late and called in sick frequently. He had a hard time adjusting to his new life of living on his own and going to school full time.

Thankfully he didn't directly answer to Andy, but that didn't mean Andy didn't notice how he was barely doing the minimum to get by. "You know," Andy said to Conor's direct supervisor after a few weeks, "feel free to treat Conor just like anybody else. It isn't doing me any favors by keeping him on if he's not doing the work." Then, to make sure she understood, he added, "You don't need my permission to fire him."

Conor wasn't fired, and Andy watched his struggles from afar. Then, one crisp October day, Conor showed up at Andy's office unannounced.

"What can I help you with, Conor?"

"Mr. Grosmaire, I'd love to go to lunch with you next week sometime."

It was a curious visit, but Andy agreed to the unexpected request. By the time their lunch meeting rolled around, Andy had gone over several scenarios in his mind. Why would Conor want to talk privately with him? He'd braced himself for the worst. Halfway through their sandwiches, Conor worked up the courage to say what he'd wanted to say to Andy.

"I'd like to ask you for Ann's hand in marriage," Conor said.

This was the "worst" Andy had feared. It's not that he didn't like Conor. In fact—after all we'd been through together—he loved the boy. But that's what he was. A boy. Though Ann and Conor had dated all through high school and now into college, he didn't appear to be growing into manhood well. Not only did he show a lack of responsibility at work, but also he'd frequently keep Ann out past her curfew and flout our household rules.

To be fair, he'd been going through a challenging time of life. First, he'd left his parents' house rather abruptly and lived with us before moving into an apartment with other college students he didn't know. But even though he was now effectively on his own, he hadn't developed the life skills required to keep a household. He lost an unhealthy amount of weight during that first semester at school, since his diet consisted of ramen noodles and Red Bull. He didn't seem to sleep well. Plus, he and his family were supposedly in counseling—but they didn't seem to go on a regular basis. We figured he'd need some time to figure out his family issues before trying to have a family of his own.

Andy took a long sip of his iced tea, trying to think of a clever response. How can a dad cloak the fact that he doesn't want his daughter to marry this person at this time? He wanted to say no, or at least that they needed to wait. But he knew that declining to give a blessing might make them more apt to run off and get married anyway.

"It's a big step, Conor," Andy said. "I'll have to think about it." But before the sentence was out of his mouth, he noticed Conor's face fall. For the rest of the meal, they picked at their food and slurped their drinks until the waitress mercifully brought their check.

When Andy got home, he and I sat on the couch to discuss all the angles.

"They're obviously not ready for marriage," I said. "Neither of them."

"What if I try to talk her out of it, but it only pushes her toward him?" Andy asked.

"You think they'll elope?" I asked.

"If we say no, then what better way to defy your parents than to run off to Vegas?"

It was true. We had laid down our curfew policy, but our rules only seemed to cause them to break them even more.

"And think of how disappointed Ann will be if we say no," I said.

We both knew it would devastate her if we "ruined" this

momentous occasion in her life. At that very time, she and Conor were probably feverishly discussing the lunch conversation from their point of view and what it meant for their future.

After we rolled the topic around for hours, Andy said, "I think it comes down to this: Do I want to be known as the father who blessed their marriage or the one who cursed it?"

We sat quietly as we contemplated the answer to that question.

⚬⚬

Wednesday morning at the hospital, we came in to a touching surprise.

"Look!" I said to Andy as we walked into the room. I stopped in my tracks. During her shift, Marie—the night nurse—had washed Ann's hair and braided it.

"I didn't even know if she still had hair!" I gasped. After all the head trauma, we assumed most of it was gone except the small part that wasn't covered by her head dressing. The braid was just a little touch of kindness, but it meant so much to us.

"How do these look?" a nurse named Pattie said, as she slipped the boots covered in thick gray fur onto Ann's feet as she lay in the bed. The special boots kept her feet bent to prevent them "freezing" in a pointed position.

"They're certainly a fashion statement, especially with that hospital gown," I said, tilting my head to consider them. "But she always wanted Uggs."

As odd as it sounds, we established a "normal life" at the hospital. We became friends with the nurses, who tended to Ann with such care and kindness.

"You guys should bring in some photos," Marie suggested Wednesday evening. "I'd love to see what Ann looked like before all this."

Her sweet request gave us the opportunity to look through pictures from cell phones and photo albums. I even found her baby "brag book," which visitors enjoyed flipping through as they sat in her room. One particular photo—of Ann pushing her sister through Costco in a large grocery cart—caused everyone to smile until the contrast to the girl asleep in the hospital bed caused the smiles to fade.

In a further effort to make Ann comfortable, we arranged her special stuffed animals around her in bed; her boss from the store placed a Sophie giraffe on her bedside table; and we tucked a hand-crocheted afghan, a graduation present from her friend Khadijah, nicely around her legs.

Visitors came and went all day in our makeshift "home." Even though the priests from Good Shepherd didn't plan to stagger their arrivals, there always seemed to be at least one of them in our conversations, in the waiting room, or by our side. Being Holy Week, it probably was the most inconvenient time for them to drop everything to be with us at the hospital. Though Easter is an important holiday for all Christian denominations, some merely consider it a special Sunday when children wear new clothes, have an egg hunt on the church property, and gorge on melted chocolate infused with blades of grass. But it's the holiest week of the year for Catholics—the high point of the liturgical calendar—and it represents the core of our faith and source of our salvation. We reorient our lives around the church, and special masses are held during the week.

Holy Week is ushered in the Sunday before Good Friday, which is known as Palm Sunday. It's a celebration of Jesus' triumphant entrance into Jerusalem when crowds welcomed, worshipped, and laid down palm leaves before him. Of course, that's not how the story ends. Holy Week contains the greatest tragedy and sorrow of the year.

The story of the arrest, trial, and suffering of Jesus is called the Passion, after a Latin word meaning "suffering." The whole week contains a certain sobriety, as the parish walks through the agony of Christ and relives the Gospel of Luke from beginning to end. Early in the week, each church in the city holds a penance service, and there are always several priests on hand for the sacrament of reconciliation, or what people commonly know as "confession."

"Would you mind hearing our confessions while you're here?" Andy asked Father Kevin, after he realized we'd not been able to make it to any of the penance services that week. Father Kevin smiled as he brought out a stole from his pocket and placed a band of colored cloth around his neck.

"Always prepared," he said, gesturing to a more private room for our individual confessions. The sacrament of reconciliation is a time for us to sit down and reflect on our lives, to admit the things we have done that don't live up to God's standards. In the book of 1 John, God instructs us about the practice: "If we confess our sins, he is faithful and just and will forgive us our sins and purify us from all unrighteousness" (1:9). After confession, the priest usually assigns some sort of penance. This is simply an action that someone can take to reestablish the relationship between the sinner and God, in order to restore God's grace.

At least that's how it is supposed to work.

Once I went to confession with the girls when they were teenagers. Father Bill, who was probably eighty years old at the time, heard the confessions of Sarah, Allyson, and Ann first.

As I entered the room, he said, "Are those your daughters?"

For a moment I hesitated. Since I had no idea what the girls had confessed, I wondered if I should I claim them. He laughed at my pause before assuring me, "They're great girls."

Relieved, I knelt down and said, "Bless me, Father, for I have sinned. It's been three months since my last confession."

"I have anger toward my husband. I don't give him the respect he deserves, and I argue with him frequently," I confessed.

"For your penance," Father Bill said, "say the Our Father twice, very slowly." In a way, penance completes the process.

Most people would've come out of the room, prayed, said their penance, and gone on with their lives. But I couldn't. More accurately, I wouldn't. Not that day. In fact, I may have left angrier than when I arrived. I had secretly hoped that after I told Father Bill why I was so angry with my husband, he would side with me or justify my anger. I imagined Andy sitting at home, not even thinking of our fight, and certainly not acknowledging that he had any fault in it. And there I was, humbling myself before God.

I was sick of being the one doing all the work! I loaded the girls into my car and went along with my errands of the day, without obeying Father Bill's instruction.

The next morning, when I woke up, I turned over and saw Andy sleeping soundly on his side of the bed. As I looked at him, oblivious to what he'd done, it dawned on me that I still hadn't done my penance. Then, with equal force, it dawned on me that I didn't care. I secretly relished the fact that I wasn't completing my penance. To do so would be to admit my wrongdoing, which somehow seemed to relieve Andy of any responsibility. No one but God knew I was in rebellion against Andy, which made it easier to maintain. I guess I hoped I could teach him a lesson, that my anger would somehow hurt him enough that he'd change. And so I pouted, considered how wrongly Andy had treated me, and congratulated myself for taking my faith more seriously than he did.

It took a lot of energy. Maintaining a steady stream of hostility, contempt, and aggression toward him did little or nothing to Andy, but it ate me up. Finally, after an entire week, I got tired of it. I got down on my knees next to my bed (though I rarely do this when praying), folded my hands together, and said the words the priest had instructed.

"Our Father who art in heaven, Hallowed be thy name," I said, very slowly. "Thy kingdom come, thy will be done on earth, as it is in heaven. Give us this day our daily bread."

As a Catholic, I'd probably recited this prayer thousands of times. We say it as a part of the mass before taking Holy Communion, the Liturgy of the Hours, and the rosary. But there was something different about saying it this time. Father Bill had instructed me to say it deliberately. Slowly. Twice.

"And forgive us our trespasses, as we forgive those who trespass against us," I said. "And lead us not into temptation, but deliver us from evil, amen."

And then, after taking a deep breath, I said it all again.

"Forgive us our trespasses, as we forgive those who trespass against us," I repeated, really spacing out the words as instructed, letting their meaning cling to me, change me.

By the time I said "amen"—the second time—God's grace washed over me. When I acknowledged my own sin without focusing on Andy's, the bitterness was taken away. Only when it was gone did I realize that God's grace had been kept from me because I was unwilling to obey and feel his forgiveness.

Forgiveness didn't come naturally to me. If doors could come off their hinges when slammed, we would've replaced all the doors at our house. I'm a really good door slammer. Many times in our marriage, my anger at Andy was probably disproportionate to the offense. At the beginning of every month—after we deposited Andy's paycheck—we'd go to Walmart and buy all our major groceries. My paycheck covered eggs, milk, and bread—all the "fill-in" groceries that need to be replenished over the course of life. My money also paid for the girls' music lessons and the extraneous things that seem to pop up all the time. Because he handled the bills, I never challenged his financial decisions; and I expected him to return the favor.

I'll never forget the time we were shopping at the beginning of the month when I picked up a box of generic Oatee O's.

"The girls like Honey Nut Cheerios," he said, picking up a brand-name box and sticking it in the cart.

"But that box costs $1.50 more."

"We can afford to get the girls the kind of cereal they want," he laughed.

"I don't think they taste that much better," I said.

"But the girls like this one," Andy repeated, and the more expensive cereal remained in the cart.

Just one aisle later, I picked up a bag of Starbucks dark roast ground coffee.

"Wait," he said, holding up a generic brand. "Here's one that's half the price."

"I thought we could occasionally splurge on the things we like," I said, putting the Starbucks into the cart, right next to the cereal to emphasize my point.

"This is just as good," Andy insisted. "We'll get this kind."

"But I like Starbucks better. We're talking about pennies per cup of coffee."

He didn't even bother to respond, but instead just reached into our cart, removed the Starbucks, and replaced it with the cheaper version.

"You're overreacting. Coffee is coffee," he said. "Why are you so upset about this?"

"You're buying Honey Nut Cheerios because that's what the girls like," I said, "but you refuse to buy the coffee I like because it's too expensive."

"But they *like the Honey Nut*," he said, in the most unassuming voice. He had absolutely no idea why this was problematic, which dumbfounded me. I didn't know how to respond, but I grew livid as I stood under those fluorescent lights.

"I'm buying the kind of coffee I want from my own checking account," I said, very slowly, holding the coffee next to me. "I'll just have the cashier ring this up separately, so you don't have to take out a loan for it."

It was the kind of argument that escalated quickly, both of us shocked that we were standing in the middle of an aisle, furious at the other. People looking for their own coffee products scooted by to give us privacy. Then the whole way home I tried to explain how it wasn't about the coffee, but how he didn't think enough of me to buy the good coffee. He never understood. For him it was only about saving money.

Another time we were shopping for a new car. As we walked through the Hyundai parking lot to the new vehicles, one of the SUVs from the used car lot caught my eye. It was a shiny, black Mercedes, and—because it was used—it was priced about the same as the new vehicles we were going to see.

"Oh, Andy," I said. "Look at that! Can we test-drive it?"

"Why do you want to test-drive a Mercedes?"

"Come on," I said. "Let's just drive it and have some fun!"

"We're not going to buy a Mercedes."

"I know. But it's here, and it's a beautiful day," I urged. "Let's just take it for a spin."

"But if you're not going to buy it," he said, "why do you want to drive it?"

"Because it's a *Mercedes*," I said, feeling that should've settled it. "I'm never going to have another chance to drive a Mercedes!"

When we got home, I slammed the door to my bedroom, flopped myself on the bed, and cried out to God.

"What am I supposed to do with him?" I asked. By this time in our marriage—after seventeen years—our relationship was stretched really thin. After I gave birth to Ann, I had another still-birth. It seemed particularly cruel for us to bury two babies. To add even more heartache, this time it was a boy we'd named Lucien. The tragedies that we'd gone through, not having a church home, and the normal wear and tear on all relationships had taken a toll. As the years went by, we had been attending church less and less. The Methodist church didn't seem to have the spirituality I was looking for. Andy and I would joke that we knew the sermon was over only after the minister had told three jokes and at least one fishing story. After going there for several years, I discovered there are twenty-six tenets of the Methodist faith, and I couldn't name one of them. I always felt like a Catholic who went to a Methodist church—never a true Methodist.

Just before Sarah entered the sixth grade, when she would have started going to the youth group, I found out from a friend that the church had a sex ed class for the youth. I'm sure part of the course was abstinence, but I was shocked to learn that they also taught them how to use birth control—just in case, in a you-know-how-kids-are-these-days type way.

Andy and I knew we couldn't attend a church that taught our daughters what we felt was our duty to teach them. In a way this incident made us take our faith more seriously, and it awakened my deep longing to return to the church of my youth.

"We need to take the girls to church," I said, after several weeks of sleeping in on Sunday. Though Andy agreed, we didn't quite live up to our aspiration of church attendance, and the weeks turned into months, which turned into years.

One fall Sunday in 1999, Andy was out of town, and I took the girls to a Catholic church named Good Shepherd for mass. We filed into a pew near the front, with the girls sitting on my left near the center aisle. We listened to the announcements—they were having a weekend retreat—and the homily. But when it came time for communion, something went awry. Ann, who was the youngest and totally unaware of how things work in a Catholic church, stood up and got in line with everyone else.

Sarah and Allyson scooted out of the pew to retrieve their sister. Somehow, and I'm still not sure how, they ended up in line as well. It was too late. We were so close to the front of church, it was all over before I could reach the end of the pew.

When I made it up to the priest, I held out my hands and he placed the host on my palm.

"The body of Christ," he said.

"Amen," I said.

But instead of the priest moving on to the person behind me, he leaned over to me and whispered, motioning to my girls. "They aren't Catholic, are they?"

I guess it was obvious they didn't know what they were doing.

Up to that point, I had been enjoying the mass. The familiar rituals and prayers. Reciting the creed and acknowledging to myself that, yes, I did believe all those things. Now, however, I went back to the pew, devastated, my face reddening with shame. My girls *were* Catholic. At least my oldest two were, because they'd been baptized in the Church. But I knew that's not what he meant.

Just because they were baptized Catholic didn't make them Catholic, any more than me attending the Methodist church had made me Methodist. My daughters really didn't know what it meant to be a member of the faith into which they had been baptized. If I didn't like the Methodist church, then I should've found another one—any other church. I should never have let my family languish for years without a spiritual anchor.

After mass, I went up to the priest.

"I just wanted to explain about what happened in there," I said. "Actually two of my daughters are, in fact, Catholic. At least, they were baptized . . ."

After he listened to my convoluted story of unrealized potential and broken vows, he simply said, "Enroll them in religious education." It wasn't an admonishment, and it wasn't a suggestion. It was a gentle commandment.

I knew it was a message straight from God.

Almost immediately, I plunged into the heart of the church. I enrolled our family as members, attended a weekend retreat, and started faithfully attending mass. Even though Good Shepherd was a place I'd never regularly attended, I finally felt I'd come home. And I couldn't help but sing out my praises louder than anyone else during the mass. Suddenly God became so alive to me that I often teared up as I sang, "Glory to God in the highest, and peace to his people on earth."

But one of my first priorities was to enroll my girls in the religious education program. They took it pretty well.

"It's an obligation that I have as your parent," I explained as they loaded up into the car to go to church for their lessons. "To bring you up in the training and instruction of the Lord."

"Aren't we already 'up'?" asked Allyson.

"How long will it last?" Ann asked.

"Well, it starts now and ends in December next year."

"We'll be in college by the time this is over," Sarah groaned.

"Listen," I said. "All kids count the weeks until summer break. This won't hurt you, and it might even be good for you."

But even as we dove headfirst into church, it added yet another issue to my relationship with Andy. When he had said he thought we should get the girls in church, I'm sure he wasn't thinking of the Catholic Church. While I had been willing to go to any church Andy wanted, neither of us really wanted to return to the Methodist church we'd been attending. By then I had no desire to search for another "compromise" church. "I feel like an outsider," Andy said to me as he saw how dedicated I'd become to the church in just a few short months. "It's like you've moved on spiritually to a church that won't even allow me to take Communion with you."

We talked—sometimes for hours—about what he thought were the Catholic Church's overly restrictive rules regarding joining the Church and participating in the Lord's Supper. Secretly, I knew Andy wouldn't feel so rejected if he didn't really want to be a part of it.

And so, we went about our spiritual lives separately. Because I was now involved in putting on a spring retreat for women, I knew that a men's weekend retreat was coming up as well. More than anything else, I wanted Andy to attend . . . not because I expected any great conversion, but rather because I felt that he had no real, deep friendships. He knew people at work, but how many of them were good Christian men? I knew I couldn't push him. So instead, I prayed. And prayed. Then, when I felt completely discouraged, I prayed some more.

"God, please open Andy's heart so that he'll go on the retreat weekend and meet good Christian men."

At the very last minute—on Thursday night—he decided to go. When he returned a couple of days later, he seemed to have had a good time. That fall, we were walking through the Walmart parking lot, back to the scene of the Honey Nut Cheerios and Starbucks showdown. I was wondering if we'd get through our grocery shopping without conflict when Andy casually said, "I'm thinking of going to that class at church you mentioned."

"Really?" I tried to maintain a nonchalance in my voice that didn't betray how much I'd prayed for this moment.

"Yeah," he said. "Just to learn."

In December 2000, Allyson and Ann made their First Communion. And on Easter Vigil in 2001, my husband and daughter Sarah became full members of the Church.

Though Andy had become a member of the Catholic Church, our troubles did not end. We decided to go to counseling to save what was left of our union.

After months of sessions, to our complete surprise, the counselor looked us straight in the eyes and delivered the bad news.

"I'll have to be honest with you," she said. "You are the most incompatible couple I've ever met. I see no option for you but divorce."

It was one thing to be furious at Andy and wonder if I could ever get along with him. It was another for a stranger to diagnose us as "incurable." Suddenly, Andy and I were united in a common cause: being furious at, then later laughing at, this counselor who was *supposed* to be helping us save our marriage. We didn't go back to her. But a united front against a wacky counselor wasn't enough to set our relationship on solid ground. Once, after Andy did something particularly offensive, I wondered how on earth we'd survive.

Was that counselor right?

"He doesn't get me, God," I prayed, after running to our bedroom, slamming the door, and burying my head in a pillow. "He'll never get me, and he's such a jerk. What am I supposed to do?"

"Forgive him."

Where did that voice come from? And anyway, why should I forgive him? How will he learn his lesson if I forgive him?

"Forgive him," said the voice again. No matter how much I argued, the answer was the same: "Forgive him."

It seemed impossible.

Then, something happened. It was one of those marital incidents between us that made me wonder, *Will we survive this? Can I forgive him?* Though I tried to suppress the incident, the pain of it lingered in my heart for several months. Finally, I asked for the help of a Catholic marriage counselor, who met with me in a chapel.

"God, please be present with us," he prayed.

We talked about the pain I was feeling, and how I couldn't shake it.

"What does God want you to know about this?"

As I sat there in the quiet chapel, I went from tears to laughter.

"What is it?" he asked.

"It's like the song," I said, and began singing, "Jesus loves me, this I know."

I heard God telling me that Andy loves me imperfectly. When I'm feeling imperfectly loved by my husband, I should remember that God loves me perfectly.

What a simple message! God loves me always.

I realized that Andy's inability to trust me—and his need for control—came from his family history, not a lack of love for me. Suddenly, a weight had been taken from my shoulders. God loves me unconditionally, and he asks me to show that sort of love toward others. Slowly, I realized something else.

I don't love Andy perfectly either.

Not only was I able to forgive Andy, but also I asked him to forgive me for not being able to love him perfectly either.

In 2005 I joined the Secular Franciscan Order, which is a community of people who pattern their lives after Christ in the spirit of St. Francis of Assisi. That meant I stood up in church and said, "It is my intention to live a gospel life."

Of course, all Christians should be living a "gospel life," but this was an intentional change, a permanent calling. In AD 1208, St. Francis showed people who weren't able to commit to the priesthood (because of family commitments or because they weren't ready to take a vow of poverty) how to live gospel-saturated lives—at home and at work—and to spread the good news of Christ among their neighbors and community. In "The Letter to All the Faithful," he wrote that we should live "a renewed life characterized by charity, forgiveness, and compassion toward others." And so, as I stood in front of the church and made my vows, I prayed.

"God, help me to be patient and to be more forgiving."

My marriage, I knew, depended on it.

Suddenly the world presented many opportunities to try out my new convictions. Very soon afterward, a church retreat planning committee was communicating via e-mail. As we discussed the itinerary for the retreat, some dissension arose among the "get up at a reasonable time" and the "sleep in" groups. When I emphasized that we should enforce "Lights Out" to encourage people to go to sleep at a reasonable hour since the wake-up call would be at 6:30 a.m., someone—perhaps intending to e-mail a smaller group of people that didn't include me—wrote, "Who does Kate think she is? We can do whatever we want. It's our retreat." And, to make it even more maddening, he insinuated he didn't want to listen to my counsel because I was a woman—even though I'd been placed in that position by Father Mike.

It boiled my blood. My instinct was to fire off an e-mail defending myself, along with a few choice words for my accuser. This time, however, I stopped, took my hands away from the keyboard, and prayed.

What does God want me to see in this e-mail?

After collecting myself, I replied to everyone with a simple message: "The retreat manual was written for a purpose, to guide us on how to do the weekends. I think Father Mike would back me up on the schedule."

The next time I saw the man at church, I could tell he was embarrassed.

"Hey," he said, approaching me cautiously. "I'm sorry about that whole e-mail thing."

"Don't worry about it," I said. "I forgive you."

It wasn't the parting of the Red Sea, but sensing God transform my heart like that was nothing short of miraculous. But here's the real miracle. Not only did I say that I forgave him, but I really—in my heart—forgave him.

From that point on, I chose as often as possible to forgive people who hurt me—from the guy who cut me off in traffic, to a rude cashier, to Andy when our arguments involve more than cereal or coffee purchases. I was becoming a forgiving person, in spite of my natural inclination toward anger. I practiced forgiveness—repeatedly—on Andy.

As I tried to live a more charitable life, my own shortcomings became even more obvious. Not only did I need to forgive; I needed forgiveness. Forgiveness became less of a commandment I was trying to follow and more of a lifestyle. My heart softened toward those who'd done wrong, especially now that I realized how much I do wrong.

I began to relish my time in confession. To non-Catholics, it might seem odd to walk into a booth and tell a priest your sins. But all Christians should take confession seriously, because it is the way forgiveness is applied.

James 5:16 says, "Confess your sins to each other and pray for each other so that you may be healed." Then, 1 John 1:9 says, "If we confess our sins, he is faithful and just and will forgive us our sins and purify us from all unrighteousness." So, as we sat in the hospital watching Ann fight for her last breaths, it was important for me to be able to confess my sins during Easter week.

I waited for Andy to come out of the small room that the Neuro ICU used as a consultation space, but which also served as a place for us to have occasional meetings. We met with the sheriff's detectives in this room and conversed with the hospital staff there. It was the size of a small office, maybe ten by ten, and had four comfortable chairs, a table with a pretty lamp, and soothing pictures on the walls. On that day it also served as our makeshift confessional booth. Normally I prepare for confession by examining my conscience and trying to be aware of everything I've done that violated God's command to love him and others by obeying his laws. This week, however, I hadn't had time to really think about my sins with all that was going on. But I said a quick prayer to the Holy Spirit, asking for guidance in the thing that was most keeping me from a full relationship with God. And an odd little thing came to mind.

I crossed myself, and began. "Bless me, Father, for I have sinned. My last confession was one month ago."

Father Kevin looked at me kindly, waiting for my confession. Honestly, as I prayed, what came to mind was theft. I'd gotten into the habit of putting Splenda in my iced tea and taking a few of the yellow packets for my purse. I knew it wasn't the worst sin in the world, but I also knew that restaurant owners across Tallahassee didn't expect to supply my sweetener needs just because I bought one drink from them.

Father Kevin is a jovial man who loves to laugh. He talks about God in simple, yet somehow deep, ways at the same time. He managed not to laugh at my big confession, but I detected a look of amusement passing over his face. Perhaps he expected some sort of angsty confession—of my lack of trust in God, of anger toward Conor, in despair over the tragedy that had come upon our house. Oddly, however, I felt closer to God that week than perhaps ever before. The church community had surrounded us, buoyed us with prayer, and loved us well.

"Anything else?" he asked, his voice full of compassion.

⁂

After lunch on Thursday, Andy went to Ann's room to find some peace and quiet after a busy morning. He knew he wouldn't have too many more opportunities to sit with her, so he valued every second. He liked to sit in her room and talk to her—about his feelings and thoughts, dealing with the family, or reading the latest comments from the online website, CaringBridge, where friends followed her progress. That afternoon, as on each one before, he prayed the daytime prayer of the Liturgy of the Hours with her. By this time, Andy realized that God was not going to heal Ann, but she was not lost to him yet. After he finished praying, he stood over Ann and listened to her steady breathing and the noise of the medical machines, looking for some sort of sign. He no longer had hope in the occasional twitch of Ann's hands or legs. They were now as routine as everything else in the room.

Father Will knocked on the door.

"May I stay and pray?" he asked. His innocent and hopeful demeanor comforted Andy, so he nodded and moved to the foot of the bed. The grief in the room was so thick that both men waited in silence. We'd decided to take Ann off any means of artificial life support the next day, so it was now a matter of hours. Andy turned back to Ann, but when he looked at her, this time he looked beyond her. *What prayers are left to say?* he wondered. *What am I still looking for?*

Father Will sat in a chair near Ann's bed. The ventilator, which both men knew would soon be turned off, whooshed rhythmically. She appeared to be asleep.

When Andy looked down at Ann's body, something happened. Instead of seeing Ann lying there in the hospital bed, he saw Christ. He looked away for a moment and shook his head. *Is this real?*

When he looked back at Ann, the vision remained.

The Lord and Ann had become one. Where he normally saw Ann's face, he saw the face of Jesus. They blended together but somehow still remained separate. Her arm trailed down to become the hand of Jesus. Both her hand and Jesus' were wrapped in bandages—they had both been pierced, one by a nail and the other by the blast of a gun. There was an overwhelming presence of peace in the room. It wasn't strong, but just ambient . . . as if it had always existed.

He saw movement in the room, but he didn't want to avert his eyes.

"Father Will," Andy whispered, "do you see?"

Father Will stood up and walked over to Andy's side. "What's going on?" he asked, sensing the urgency in Andy's voice.

Andy motioned to the bed. "I see Jesus lying there in the bed. Do you see him? But Ann is there too."

"I don't see it," he said. "What else do you see? Both Jesus and Ann right here?"

"I don't see two distinct people," Andy said. "They're one and the same. I can't tell where her body ends and Jesus' begins. They're the same."

"Jesus is here?"

"There!" He pointed to the bed.

Father Will leaned forward with a gentle and tender offering at the foot of the hospital bed, of the cross. He kissed the feet of Ann and Jesus. He moved to their bandaged hands and kissed them. He leaned forward and kissed the wounds on their heads. Andy was overwhelmed with a new sense of love in the room, as he watched Father Will touch the wounds of Christ, just as Thomas had touched Jesus' wounds thousands of years ago. He recognized this person in the bed as someone to whom he'd given his life.

What else can you do in the presence of God?

Andy's whole body began to rejoice and sing. He said he never felt more fully alive, as all the angst and sorrow of the past few days were temporarily replaced by an intense joy and happiness. He gazed onto the body of Christ, realizing that he'd misunderstood what had happened on Monday at two o'clock in the morning. He had believed he was having an "argument" with Ann over forgiving Conor. However, it wasn't Ann at all. Jesus was the one asking Andy to forgive Conor.

It was God himself.

This penetrated his heart. When God asked him to forgive, it carried much more gravity than when Ann had been the one requesting it. Andy started crying, but not tears of sadness. Tears of joy flowed from his eyes as Jesus was asking him to do something.

Forgive.

The answer was yes. Andy forgave Conor right then and there, and not with the reluctant kind of forgiveness he'd proffered to Ann in exasperation a few nights before. Andy had never said no to Jesus before. Why would he start then?

A sense of awe overcame Andy, and he fell to his knees. Tears of happiness rolled down his face. Father Will knelt beside him and put his hand on his shoulder. Andy bowed his head and thanked and praised God for his love and mercy.

"Lord, how tender and merciful you are with me to come and show me what is so evident. You've always been with Ann. When she couldn't speak, you spoke for her. How blind I've been not to recognize what's so evident now. You've been and always will be one with her as she is now with you." He felt Father Will hug him, and he realized that if Jesus was one with Ann, then he must also be one with Conor. "Yes, I will be obedient to what you ask," he said. "Yes, I'll forgive Conor."

When he raised his head, he looked back to the hospital bed.

There, he saw only Ann, and he heard the whoosh of the machines once again.

⌘

Before we left the hospital that night, we shared with the nurses our decision to remove Ann from the ventilator the following day. As the neurosurgeon had predicted, her organs were failing. We received the news that day that her pituitary gland was shutting down, causing other systems to fail. We had to face the inevitable.

That evening we were in Ann's bedroom discussing how things would go on Friday. I couldn't stop thinking about the fact that my name was scrawled on a list somewhere at the Leon County jail. I'd decided to go visit Conor.

Even more than that, I'd decided to forgive him.

It had started on Tuesday evening, when the McBrides came to see us. I'd said, "We don't define Conor by that one moment." For some reason, as I said those words, they reinforced in my head what I was feeling in my spirit.

I had forgiven the man who shot my daughter.

Of course, this was in keeping with the vows I'd taken at church—to live a life of patience, charity, and forgiveness . . . a life "worthy of the gospel." But I had no idea how Andy, the big bear of a daddy, would feel if I went to the jail and offered forgiveness to the person who changed our family forever.

I wasn't even sure if I could say the words, but I knew—at a very deep level—it was true.

"I'm going to see Conor tomorrow."

"Really?" Andy said.

"I want to see him before Ann dies," I said. I definitely didn't want to be the one to break the news that his fiancée had died. "I think it'd be simpler."

Andy nodded.

"Is there anything you want me to tell him?" I asked hesitantly.

"Actually, yes," he said, looking at me. "Tell him I love him and forgive him."

CHAPTER 8

*T*here was a line.

I stood in front of an older man wearing a faded Florida Gators T-shirt. A Hispanic couple, murmuring in Spanish, stood behind me while looking over their passports.

Visitation started at 9:00 a.m., and I planned my arrival time to coincide. The night before, Andy and I had managed to attend a Holy Thursday service—the only Easter-related service we could make. Ann was shot on Palm Sunday, and our struggles seemed to be growing, unfolding, and swelling along with the story of Christ's Passion. By this time on the morning of Good Friday—the actual Good Friday—Christ had just spent the night in prison. As I stood there in the Leon County jail, nervously wondering what awaited me inside, I could easily imagine the Messiah in his cell. Stone. Dark. Alone. Christ's imprisonment felt real to me for the first time.

The man in the Florida Gators T-shirt moved ahead in line, so I shuffled forward as well. I wondered if Christ had visitors. His disciples may have tried to be with him, but the men surely left. Were the women, so culturally insignificant, allowed to stay? Did someone tend to Christ before his death?

I pushed these thoughts out of my mind. To my left, about a dozen people sat in plastic chairs, while a television screen up in the corner flickered the latest news. Apparently they were waiting because the jail was divided into pods. Only so many visitors were allowed in each pod during a certain time period. A man stuck some coins into a vending machine to get a soda, a child in a chair ate chips, and everyone else mindlessly watched the screen. On my right, another room had a row of chairs facing each of two walls. In front of each chair was a television monitor. Several people talked with prisoners on the screen. Apparently, some visitors could go inside the prison and see the prisoner through the thick glass, but others could only teleconference over the screen. I wanted to get as close to Conor as possible.

A hallway, maybe about fifteen feet wide, yawned before me. On one side of it, visitors placed their belongings in a plastic basket before walking through the metal detector.

"They will only allow you to have your car key and driver's license," Julie had warned me. "Everything else you should leave in the car, or you can use a locker in the waiting room." My car would do fine.

In the middle, a woman sat at a desk that came up high, all the way to my chest. It was rounded at the front and went back into the hallway, making a long horseshoe.

"Next," she said, nodding toward me.

"I'm here to see Conor McBride," I said. I handed her my driver's license as I'd seen the man in the Gators T-shirt do earlier. Then I took a deep breath.

She tapped my name into the computer, but then sat up in her chair. Her eyes darted from the screen to my driver's license, back to the screen, and then squarely at me.

"Are you the victim's mother?"

"I am," I said, my stomach churning.

"Step over here for a minute," she instructed. It was neither kind nor harsh, but I could tell by her tone that I was not her typical visitor. I understood her reticence. Being there felt unnatural for me too. Almost otherworldly. "I need to call my supervisor," she said.

I stood there for what felt like an hour, though it was probably about two minutes. Eventually, a short woman dressed in a Leon County Sheriff's uniform approached with my driver's license in her hand. She was frowning.

"Kate Grosmaire?"

I nodded.

"You're here to see the man who shot your daughter?"

"Yes."

She paused, the moment full of unspoken protestations.

"Well, you're on his list and you have your ID with you," she said, "so I'm going to let you go up."

"Thank you," I said.

"But let me warn you," she said, eyeing me seriously. "I don't want you pounding on the glass."

"I'm not here to pound on the glass," I said.

She led me to a wall where they snapped a photo of me, printed it out on a sticker, and wrote a time on it—half an hour from the moment it came out of the printer. "This tells you when you're supposed to be back," she said. "Don't be late, or else the prisoner's visitation privileges will be suspended for the rest of the month."

She handed me a badge with a pod number and directions to Conor's pod. I had exactly thirty minutes—including the time it took me to walk up to the pod and back through the labyrinth of hallways. The corridor's glass windows let in the morning sun, which made the un-air-conditioned hallways warm and suffocating. The concrete floor and the cinderblock walls reverberated with a harsh echo upon every step.

At the end of the hall, I came to a small entryway next to a bank of elevators. I pressed the number printed on my badge and noticed Conor's pod was designated as a medical pod. For a moment, I wondered why he'd be there, until I remembered. Michael had told us he was under suicide watch. I walked down another cinderblock hallway and noticed a room through a big glass window. Inside, a couple of officers, sitting in front of a row of screens, monitored everything going on in the pods. They opened the heavy metal door, which was layered with drips of hard, brown paint, and I walked into a room with an intercom.

"I'm here to see Conor McBride," I said into the little box.

"One moment," a voice from the other side said.

I couldn't believe the inefficiency of this system. Not only did I have to spend precious visitation minutes walking to the pod; but also the officers didn't even call him until this moment. I looked around the room, trying not to think about the ticking clock. The room was divided into four areas—each with a plastic bucket chair with metal legs in front of a plexiglass partition. Miniature walls between each visiting area gave one the impression of privacy, though the chairs were very close together, and—presumably—the officers in the other room were observing every movement and recording every word. I'm sure they'd been warned: *Watch this one. She's the victim's mom.* On the right-hand side in each area was a phone.

"I want you to know . . ." I whispered to myself. I had prepared a speech for Conor, one I hoped to have the composure to deliver.

I was on the second floor, and from one angle in the pod, I could see down to the first floor. There was an area with chairs and a sofa facing a television. A cafeteria table sat in front of another glass wall, which had a small recreational room behind it. A man was shooting hoops alone at a basketball goal. To the far left, a door led to a grassy area. To my right was a row of metal doors with small glass windows. Cells.

Against the backdrop of the sun pouring in through the glass wall, I could see the outline of a man coming toward me. I could only really see his silhouette, but I'd know Conor anywhere. He'd had some muscle damage in his legs when he was young, which made him sort of swing one of his legs. As he got closer, I noticed he was wearing a bluish-gray jail uniform. When Andy visited weeks later, he told me he had expected a monster to walk up. Conor would have raggedy teeth, long fingernails, and be drooling—because only a monster could do something this terrible. Unlike Andy, I wasn't expecting some scary apparition. I expected someone who'd made a terrible mistake. That's just what I got.

He sat down on the other side of the glass. When our eyes met, his eyes immediately filled with tears. So did mine. He picked up the phone. I picked up the phone.

"I'm so sorry," he said, beginning to sob. "I'm so, so, so sorry."

"I know," I said, putting my hand up to the glass in my desire to connect with him in some way. It must've seemed so corny, since this dramatically futile gesture happens in every fictional jail-visitation scene. Conor instinctively reached out, placing his hand on the other side of the glass. Even as our hands rested just millimeters away from each other, I realized it didn't count. The glass was smooth and transparent, but it was primarily a divider. We made an effort to reach each other, but we couldn't connect in any meaningful way.

"How is Ann?" he asked.

"She's holding her own," I said.

Holding her own was the phrase I'd chosen—an ambiguous expression that could apply to a boxer in a ring, a toddler with the flu, or a politician in a hotly contested race. I figured it could also apply to a teenager who would soon be disconnected from her life support. But I didn't tell Conor that.

The guards in the monitoring room were probably sitting on the edge of their chairs, watching with bated breath, and wondering, *What is she gonna say to him?* I got the feeling that they were waiting for me to lose it, to start screaming and pounding on the glass. They may have assumed they'd need to pull me out of the room. As I looked at Conor, my rehearsed speech evaporated from my memory, so I began with the one thing I knew I was supposed to convey.

"Mr. Grosmaire wants me to tell you he loves you and he forgives you," I said. Conor's eyes widened a bit. Could he trust what he was hearing? Of course, Andy had it easy. He'd expressed his sentiment to me at home. He didn't have to look Conor in the eye and form the words.

"Conor," I began. I definitely wanted to forgive him, but I just didn't know—in the moment—if my body would cooperate. "You know I love you." At the word *love*, my voice broke. By this time, tears were falling down my cheeks. I cleared my throat. "And I forgive you."

I did it, I thought with much satisfaction. God's presence empowered me to say what I needed to say, what I wanted to say. When the words actually made it out of my mouth, Conor dropped his head, folded over into himself, and wept.

"I forgive you." Saying that sentence created a bigger reality into which I could step. Up until this point, I'd felt it. I'd thought it. But now, having said it out loud, I knew it was true. In that moment, I put on forgiveness, and it was even more a part of me than when I'd walked into the jail.

Shortly after I told Conor that Andy and I both forgave him, a woman came in and sat down at one of the other phones. When her significant other arrived, I expected it might be awkward to overhear a loving conversation that would've been private in an ideal circumstance.

Of course, this was not an ideal circumstance.

When her boyfriend showed up, she let him have it.

"I can't believe you got arrested!" she shrieked. "What did you think you were doing?"

He hung his head, without saying a word.

"We have bills to pay! We need money!" she yelled. "How are we going to pay these bills? How am I supposed to buy groceries?"

Again, no response.

"You're sitting in here, and I'm out here. What am I supposed to do?"

Conor and I continued to talk, but I wasn't allowed to ask for details of the day Ann was shot. Not only was it difficult to talk through the glass; now this woman's screams drowned out whatever awkward conversation we conjured. Even though the entire Leon County Sheriff's office had been eavesdropping on our conversation, there was just something intrusive about having others in that room with us. I knew, and he knew, that we'd had our moment.

Because we couldn't talk, Conor and I just looked at each other as we listened to her screed. Finally, in the absurdity of the moment, we couldn't help it. We both started laughing. Our intimate spiritual experience of forgiveness and love had been interrupted by the most angry, profanity-laced tirade imaginable.

Suddenly, it all seemed so very awkward. Laughing when our reality was miles away from funny.

"I better get back downstairs. Good-bye, Conor," I said. I hung up the phone, turned, and walked out of the room.

∽

I arrived at the hospital at nearly eleven o'clock, where a few friends had gathered. I'd sent out word that we'd be taking Ann off life support, so people—out of respect—gave us our privacy.

The nurse came into the waiting room and went over the procedure with us again. "Ann will be removed from the ventilator,
then we'll transfer her to the hospice floor," she said. "There's room
for family there, room to stretch out."

"Then what happens?" Andy asked.

"Then, you wait."

"How long?"

"It's hard to know. Hours, days? We can't be sure," she said.

Hours, days . . .

I remembered when they briefly had removed her from the
vent a few days before. It had been such a struggle for her to draw a
breath. Her whole upper body heaved over and over in a laborious
effort to live. That test had only lasted a minute. Now it might be
hours, days? How were we supposed to sit with her and watch that
struggle? Yet I knew I would be by her side until the last, whatever
it took.

It was April 2. Sarah's birthday was April 4, and I didn't want
Ann to die on her sister's birthday. Sarah and Allyson were there,
along with Janis, Kathleen, and Ann's best friend Khadijah. Father
Mike, Father Chris, and Father Will were once again all there.

"May I go in to say good-bye?" Khadijah asked.

"Of course," I said.

We stayed in the small waiting room, which had grown quiet
now. The silence was interrupted by a gentle knock on the door—
the music minister for the hospital. She was a young woman, with
a guitar slung over her shoulder and a little notepad.

"Do you mind?" she asked, motioning to a chair. "I thought I
might come by and play songs while you're in the hospice room." I
looked at her—she couldn't have been more than thirty years old.
But there she was, confident, caring, and offering up her God-
given talent to simply help us in our moment of grief.

"Are there any specific songs that you would like for me to play?"

FORGIVING MY DAUGHTER'S KILLER

"Do you happen to know 'Angel Band'?"

She bit her lip. "Sorry," she said, jotting down the name of the song in her notebook. Though O *Brother, Where Art Thou?* was a popular movie at the time, most people wouldn't necessarily know that song off the top of their head. I, however, knew it backward and forward because I played the soundtrack frequently in the car. Since it was Ann's favorite hymn, she would put that song on repeat as I drove her to school in the mornings.

Khadijah was gone for a long time. Her father had died just a few years before, and she had struggled with her grief. Since Ann and Khadijah had the same classes at school that semester, Ann helped her with all her homework assignments. Her assistance allowed Khadijah to keep up with her academics while her personal life was so challenging. After she came back to the waiting room, Sarah and Allyson went in for their time by themselves with their sister. We don't know what they talked about, but when we went into the room afterward, Ann had a dollar bill tucked into her hand. Payment of an old debt? The ferryman's fee?

As we waited for a hospice room to become available, I became more anxious. Then, suddenly, it was time to remove Ann from the ventilator.

Father Mike had to return to Good Shepherd. On Good Friday many Catholic churches hold a stations service at three o'clock, the hour that Christ died. The stations of the cross recount his final Passion, from "Jesus is condemned to death" to "Jesus is laid in the tomb." It is a solemn reminder of his sacrifice for us.

Slowly we filed into Ann's room to say bedside prayers: Father Chris and Father Will, her aunts Teresa and Patti, her grandmother, Andy, and me. The room didn't seem crowded, as we all just took a place at her bedside. I stood on her left side and held her uninjured left hand. One of the nurses was there as well as the respiratory therapist.

When the palliative care doctor arrived, the respiratory therapist walked over to the ventilator. It was a large machine with a number of flashing buttons and digital readouts. Over the week, I had learned about the machines and how to interpret some of the numbers. Her heart rate; her pulse ox, which measured how much oxygen her lungs were able to send into her blood; and her respirations, carefully controlled by the ventilator. I had learned to recognize what the nurses had called "riding the vent"—those times when the machine was doing all the work—and the other times, when Ann's body was drawing in air on its own. A yellow line indicated the sharp intake of a breath and the slow release of another, then another. A rhythmic whooshing was constantly in the background.

The respiratory therapist turned off the machine. The indicator lights all went out, and the ventilator deflated and remained still at the bottom of its chamber. No click signifying a new breath. Only silence and a dark screen. I was shocked by how immediate and complete it was. On television there's a beep-beep-beep indicating a heartbeat and a digital display that slowly counts down the end of life into a flat line. But in real life, there was no visual sign, no auditory signal. No line jumping up and down on the screen, one heartbeat slowly distancing itself from the next.

No, just silence.

Quickly, silently, professionally, the therapist removed the tape attaching the ventilator tube to Ann's face, and in one swift motion she pulled the tube out and placed it out of sight. With no sound, it was if the room was frozen. Everyone stood completely still. The spell was broken by the nurse, who turned to Father Will and said, "Isn't there something you want to do? If so, you need to do it now."

It slowly sank in. Ann was not heaving as she did with her breathing test before. Her breaths were shallow, barely even noticeable. Father Will walked from the foot of the bed to stand next to me, taking the space left vacant by the technician. He opened his Bible to 1 Kings, chapter 19, and read about the prophet Elijah, who begged God to take his life. He was hiding from his enemies in a desert under a broom tree.

"He came to a broom bush," read Father Will, "sat down under it and prayed that he might die. 'I have had enough, LORD,' he said. 'Take my life'" (v. 4).

Father Will then read to us that Elijah fell asleep. When he awoke, an angel touched him. "Get up and eat," the angel said, "for the journey is too much for you" (v. 7).

After Father Will read the words of the angel, he took a small medicine bottle with a dropper out of his jacket pocket. Part of the last rites administered to the dying is one last Communion, or the viaticum, which means "strength for the journey."

Ann's mouth was slightly open. When Father Will leaned over and placed a few drops on her tongue, her tongue seemed to reach out to receive it. We all looked at one another with wide eyes, so surprised at the purposeful movement.

I rearranged her hand in mine so I could feel her pulse. It wasn't strong, but it was steady. I looked at her face. She looked so peaceful, I could have easily imagined she was sleeping in some Saturday morning before heading off to work. But all her work was done. The rhythmic beating of her pulse began to slow.

This was it.

Now.

We won't have to move her, I thought. *It won't be prolonged.* I felt her pulse weaken and slow. Dr. Sheedy, the palliative doctor, took Father Will's spot and placed his stethoscope over Ann's heart. Her pulse grew faint. I could feel her hand begin to cool in mine. Her face was pale. Dr. Sheedy glanced up at the clock.

"Three twenty-five p.m.," he said, and the nurse made a note of the time.

After announcing the time of death, Dr. Sheedy stepped away.

"May I hold her?" Andy asked through his tears. He came around to where the doctor had been standing and practically climbed into the hospital bed. He picked her up, drew her into his chest, and sobbed.

In that moment the song came to me. We all stood silently, as Andy held her and cried.

How could I sing at a time like this? Since Sunday night, I knew this moment was coming . . . that it was coming no matter what. It was right to let her go. It was right to send her off with a song, her favorite gospel song.

The room had become so quiet, so silent. It begged for something to fill the silence.

Everyone in the room had a different experience of loss and grief. My sister Patti says that she saw angels come and carry Ann's soul up to heaven. I felt that my daughter was already gone, and just her body remained. Perhaps just a thread remained, because I know I saw that last purposeful movement to receive Communion. I guess we don't really know what happens at the point of death, when the soul is liberated from the body that had housed it here on earth.

I just know at that moment, I was calm. It had been a chaotic, shocking week. Then, her death was all so very peaceful. And in that calmness, I sang.

"My latest sun is sinking fast . . ."

I sang the first verse and paused just a moment for the words of the second verse to come to me. When I finished, the last note hung in the air for a moment, followed by a brief silence.

"May I have a lock of her hair?" I asked the nurse.

"No," she said sadly. "I'm so sorry, but Ann's body is evidence."

"Her hair?" I asked, fighting a tidal wave of emotion. "Her braid?" She nodded.

We left the Neuro ICU to tell those in the waiting room that Ann had died. When I returned to the room to collect her things—and to say good-bye one more time—the nurse came up to me and handed me a small cloth bag.

"Here," she said. "It's her braid. I'll deal with the medical examiner if he has any questions."

And just like that, Conor's charge was changed to murder. In fact, the grand jury later charged him with murder in the first degree.

CHAPTER 9

*A*ndy and I settled into the booth at Starbucks. I stirred the Splenda in my coffee—one packet, leaving the rest for other customers. My friend Doris gazed at me across the table, her notebook open. She had barely touched her cheese Danish.

"Have you thought about what songs you'd like during the service?" she asked. As the head of Good Shepherd's bereavement ministry, Doris was good at gently leading us through the process without pushing an agenda or checking items off a list.

To my delight, about five people from the men's choir agreed to learn "Angel Band," complete with a banjo and a hammered dulcimer, before the service. I also asked them to sing "All Creatures of Our God and King" during the service. And Andy had run into Pascale Shaftel, Ann's high school French teacher, and she had asked if there was anything she could do.

"Actually, would you sing at her funeral mass?" Andy asked. Pascale is French Canadian and is trained as an opera singer. Her husband is the minister of music at Good Shepherd, and Andy had heard her sing "Ave Maria" once before. In fact, he'd already told me he wanted her to sing it at his funeral. To our delight, she'd agreed to sing it for Ann's.

"Have you thought about who will do the Scripture readings?" Doris asked.

Her little checklist included everything we needed to decide for a proper service. A funeral mass follows a certain pattern, so we didn't have to come up with a format. There would be an entrance song, a Communion song, an offertory song, three Scripture readings, the prayers of the faithful, and the distribution of Communion.

"I already asked my mom," I said. "My main concern is family members getting up and sobbing so much they can't make it to the end of the passage."

"Can she do it?" Doris was as pragmatic as an insurance salesperson, but as gentle as a fluffy pillow. She led me through the questions in a loving, practical way—and not only because she's a lovely Southern lady. She had lost her husband about three years before, and I believe her widowhood gave her more compassion and sensitivity for others who grieved.

"She *said* she could." I smiled.

"Well, you won't believe it, but someone called the church and offered to read a passage," she said.

Without her even having to tell me, I knew it was Barbara Palmer, the wife of the ophthalmologist who tried to assist Ann in the hospital. She was one of the readers at our church, and she took the Word of God seriously. I loved her passion, and how she always said she was "preaching" when she read the holy Scriptures.

"Perfect," I said, exchanging a look with Andy. We had already considered asking Barbara if she would be willing to read.

"Who's going to give the eulogy?" she asked. The funeral was planned for exactly one week after Ann died, because of the Easter holiday and travel issues. We had more time than most people to plan, but we couldn't pin down one of the most important aspects of the service.

"We'll have to get back to you on that."

First, we asked Rod Durham, a high school drama teacher who was like her second father. During those rocky high school years—when kids naturally separate from parents—Rod was a trustworthy presence in her life. Their relationship provided a safe and honest place to ask questions and figure out what sort of adult she wanted to be. Unfortunately, the drama class was on spring break in Tampa for the state drama competition after Easter. None of the drama students would be at the funeral, and Rod had to decline.

Second, we asked Molly Shakar, Ann's boss at the baby boutique. She had an interesting perspective on Ann as well, since she had gotten to know her through the store. She saw Ann pay sweet attention to the mothers and their children, and she trusted Ann to open and close the store as an eighteen-year-old. But she declined too. "I couldn't get through the eulogy without weeping," she said. "There's just no way I can do it."

As we sat there wondering whom to ask next, I looked at Andy and said, "We should do it."

"What are you thinking?" he laughed. "We can't do it."

"Who else?" I asked. We knew her better and had loved her longer than anyone. Secretly, I figured I'd do a much better job than anyone else.

"Well, let's start writing it," Andy said, though he had his doubts. "And if it's too much, we can get someone else to read it."

We sat down together with my laptop and started writing. My hands paused above the keyboard. "Where do you start on a eulogy?"

"At the beginning, I guess."

"We didn't know she would be a girl—we *knew* she would be a girl. We gave her her name, Ann Margaret, the day after she was born. Before that, we hadn't been able to agree on a name—Andy and I hadn't. Sarah and Allyson knew what they wanted to name her: Rainbow Dolphin Star Heart. That would have been some name to grow up with."

We smiled and cried as the words flowed out of us and onto the screen.

"You know what?" I said about an hour—and a thousand words—later. "I can do this. I know I can."

"Really, Kate?"

"All I need is for you to stand behind me," I said. "I'll read it until I can't."

∽

The day of April 10, 2010, was like any other spring day in Florida: warm and sunny, without a single cloud in the sky. Before people started arriving for the service, we went upstairs to see the church. There, next to Ann's ashes, was an oil portrait that stopped me in my tracks.

"Look, Andy!" I gasped. "Who did this?" As it turned out, the funeral home had taken one of the photos we'd submitted of Ann and made it into a jaw-dropping portrait. We were totally blown away by their thoughtfulness and kindness. The photo had come from her most recent birthday. The artist had simply removed her party hat, and kept her gorgeous smile.

Happier days.

I stood there for a moment, admiring the painting . . . trying to get lost in her eyes. Though the artist had done a magnificent job at capturing Ann's essence, I had to stop looking at it. Her eyes were just layers of paint, though perfectly applied. I couldn't really look into them.

"God," I prayed, interrupting the rare moment of silence before the activity of the day began, "get us through this."

We went down to the basement of the family center to await the funeral. We milled around, straightening ties, grabbing Kleenex, preparing for all the people who were beginning to arrive. Cruelly, it felt a little like a wedding—all my family gathered in nice clothes, awaiting a ceremony involving Ann and—in an odd way—Conor. Though he was locked away in the Leon County jail, we had gathered because of him. I remembered the angst we'd felt over Conor's request to marry Ann. We'd agonized over how to handle that situation perfectly, so we wouldn't alienate either of them. Our hesitance was warranted, but we never could have imagined this.

About fifteen minutes before the funeral, someone from the church rushed down the stairs, a little out of breath.

"The CBS affiliate news station just arrived," he said. "They asked me what their limitations are."

"What do you mean?" Andy asked. "What do they want to do?"

"They want to know if they can film the funeral," he said. "And if you don't want them to film the funeral, can they film anything else?"

"Why do we have to deal with this now?" I asked. "Right now before the funeral starts?"

"If you'd like me to tell them to leave," he said, "I will."

We never answered the *Tallahassee Democrat*'s phone calls, responded to the TV stations' requests, or interviewed with *People* magazine. We had no desire to do that, to be so public with our grief during this time, to make the tragedy the story.

Andy and I discussed our options and decided to let them stay.

"Tell them they can come inside the church, but no cameras," Andy said. "Tell them to respect the church service and no interviews."

I tried to shake off that unexpected development. But when we came into the sanctuary, I saw the reporter with her cameraman, sitting in the foyer of the church, a notebook in her lap. Even if she hadn't been taking notes, I would have been able to pick her out immediately. They were the only people in the packed room I didn't know.

The family settled in on the front rows, and I grabbed Andy's hand. The men's choir began singing "Angel Band," which cut me straight to the core. Their version was touching, beautiful. I couldn't believe they could so quickly learn a song not typically performed at mass. The banjo and the dulcimer echoed through the church, hitting notes of hope even among the mourning. Then Dr. Joe played "Clare de Lune" on the piano. After a few moments of silence, I knew it was time.

This was it.

"As our sister Ann has died in the Lord," Father Will began, "so may she live with him in glory." We were touched that seven priests and four deacons celebrated the mass, although Father Will was the main celebrant.

I had carefully chosen the message in the scriptures.

From Revelation 21:4: "'He will wipe every tear from their eyes. There will be no more death' or mourning or crying or pain."

And from John 12:24–25: "Very truly I tell you, unless a kernel of wheat falls to the ground and dies, it remains only a single seed. But if it dies, it produces many seeds. Anyone who loves their life will lose it, while anyone who hates their life in this world will keep it for eternal life."

Father Will did the homily, in which he brought out how Ann's death echoed the death of Christ. He explained how the whole parish was brought into the reality of the Passion that week like none other. Ann was shot on Palm Sunday, which began Passion Week. She faced death during the week and even passed away on Good Friday—the same day and the same hour as Christ had died. The way he described it elevated her death from some horrible tragedy to a sacred suffering, echoing Christ's. There was a difference, though. Christ was perfect and sinless. The Savior of the world.

He suffered because of our sins and would rise again, triumphant over death. Sadly Ann's death was not reversible, but we knew that she—as a believer—would be able to benefit in his victory.

In fact, 1 Corinthians 15 says, "'Death has been swallowed up in victory' . . . He gives us the victory through our Lord Jesus Christ" (vv. 54, 57).

I felt that eternal hope of being reunited with Ann one day as I listened to Father Will speak. After Communion, the familiar piano introduction to "Ave Maria" began. Throughout our planning, we had wanted the music in Ann's service to express God's love, care, and provision for us. As Pascale began singing, we knew we'd succeeded.

"Ave Maria, gratia plena . . ." The crowd sat in rapt attention as she sang. *"Dominus tecum* . . ."

When she sang the last note, I knew it was time to see if I could get through the eulogy—contrary to Andy's doubts. I walked up to the pulpit, my husband positioned right behind me.

I cleared my throat.

"We didn't know she would be a girl—we *knew* she would be a girl . . . Sarah and Allyson knew what they wanted to name her: Rainbow Dolphin Star Heart." Everyone laughed, eager to find some levity, some bright spots in a service commemorating the life and death of someone so young.

"That would have been some name to grow up with. She loved her older sisters, Sarah and Allyson, and missed them terribly when they went to school."

I looked out on the first rows, looked at her sisters, and smiled. They were crying.

"Her love extended from the smallest to the largest of animals . . . No matter what career path she followed, her ultimate goal was to find a piece of land where she could raise horses and rescue birds of prey."

So far I'd kept my part of the deal. My voice was smooth and clear, unadulterated by any emotion trying to sneak in and sabotage my delivery. I knew I could cry later in the privacy of my home without everyone being held hostage by a public breakdown.

"Our family shared many camping adventures together, and once grown, Ann continued to share adventures with her sister Allyson. Over the past summers, they have taken trips to Providence Canyon in Georgia and to South Carolina, where they entertained the most unusual guests by the campfire—wild pigs."

I loved that the girls continued to hang out together as adults. I had been looking forward to seeing their relationships as they all had children, to watching "Aunt Ann" take care of her nieces and nephews armed with knowledge she'd gleaned from working at the baby boutique.

"At her job, she'd send us pictures of the latest sleepers and laboring gowns. We never quite understood her love of Sophie the giraffe, a soft squeaky toy teether. But I think that sweet little face just grows on you.

"Ann sought Jesus in her own unconventional way. Ultimately, it was Ann who led us back to our Catholic faith."

I told the story of how I'd brought the girls to church, and Ann had popped up to get Communion even though she wasn't Catholic. Everyone laughed when I told them that the priest had leaned over and asked me about the girls: "They aren't Catholic, are they?"

It's one of my favorite stories, because it shows how Ann sought her faith in a real and tangible way. She didn't care about whether or not her actions were technically correct—she wanted to get to God and she did, unknowingly drawing the rest of the family toward him as well.

"It is our faith and God's grace that have gotten us through these past weeks," I said. At this point, my voice finally began to break. Looking out into the audience of people—everyone we'd ever known in Tallahassee, from work, from school, from church, from the community—I was overcome by emotion. And so, I stepped aside from the microphone. Seamlessly, Andy stepped up and began reading. He didn't miss a syllable; he didn't pause to find his place. He spoke confidently.

"We love Conor, and we cannot define him by that one moment. Because if we do, then we also define Ann by that moment. The doctor said it was a miracle that she was alive when she arrived at the hospital. It was. Because if she had died before that, then her death would have been one of violence. Instead, we all had the opportunity to see her, spend time with her, say good-bye to her, and witness her most peaceful death."

Andy's voice was smooth and calm. As he read a section, it allowed me the time to gather myself and regain control of my emotions.

"We want to conclude with words Ann wrote herself on June 6, 2009," I said, taking the paper back from Andy. We'd found this writing of Ann's in a small book in her room.

"'I am Ann Margaret Grosmaire. I am eighteen years old. I am an adult. I have entered the real world—finally after seventeen years of waiting and wondering. My childhood is a stage of my life best kept separate from my adulthood. It is behind me now. There is no sense in letting it disturb my adulthood. Now is the time for growth. To my best ability I will continue to add to myself. I know no fear, only curiosity and a true sense of self. I need not impress. I need not approval. I am self-enriching—not self-doubting. I live a simple life. It is so simple it could almost be labeled boring and dull. This doesn't bother me. I'm often alone. This leads me to be quiet. I enjoy quiet. I enjoy simple. Drama is only a hassle. Problems are things I wish to avoid. Emotions lead only to trouble. The unknown is waiting to be discovered. The future may be shaped, but the past never changed. The present is to live in, for soon as it is, it is gone. In ink which cannot be erased, I will record the events in my life that cannot be changed.'

"That ink has now been placed on paper, not in this world but in heaven in the Book of Life," I said, realizing that Andy and I had just made it. We'd eulogized our youngest daughter, our love. And we'd done a pretty good job too.

"Thank you very much."

∽

"We're having a program to honor Ann," Rod Durham said over the phone. "Can you come?"

While the funeral at Good Shepherd was packed full of friends and loved ones, there was one noticeably absent group: Ann's theater peers. On that day, the Leon Thespians were in Tampa for state competition, so at 2:00 p.m.—the exact time our service started—the drama troupe formed a circle at the hotel to honor her. As soon as everybody was back in town on Tuesday night, the teens wanted to share their memories with us.

We were deeply touched that they wanted to remember Ann, but we weren't sure what to expect when we arrived at the small auditorium classroom. It began with the song "We Shall Walk Through the Valley in Peace." Then two of her friends, Colin and Casey, gave short but touching eulogies about how she was a behind-the-scenes helper as a student director, a member of the technical crew, and a stage manager.

When she was a senior, Ann came out from the background and was persuaded to be one of the main characters in the play *Proposals*. That year, she won the Thespian of the Year Award, which would be named "Ann Grosmaire Thespian of the Year" in her honor after we created a drama scholarship.

"She was quiet, but when she talked," Casey said, "people respected her." It was so moving to hear what a good friend Ann had been to Casey. Afterward, they sang "The Rose" and finished with Sarah Folsom singing "Angel." The way this memorial would work was simple. Each person had thought of one word to describe their friend, which they'd say as they lit one of the tea lights on the table at the front.

The first student came up to the table, grabbed the lighter, and ignited the little wick. "Witty."

Another walked up, lit the next candle, and simply said, "Beautiful."

The next: "Reliable."

It was very powerful in its simplicity. Though they were drama students, this was no performance. After about the fifth student went to the table, lit the candle, and uttered his one-word tribute, I suddenly thought: *We're not recording this. I won't remember this. I'm not writing this down. I'll forget the words.*

"Funny," a student said.

"Loyal," said another.

"Considerate."

The words were so beautiful, so poignant. I told myself to enjoy the experience instead of worrying about documenting it. I remember thinking every parent of a teenager would want to hear their teen described by their friends in this way—maybe for graduation or another significant milestone.

Honestly, I'd sometimes get frustrated at Ann for staying so late at her play practices. She'd be at school until ten or eleven o'clock at night, then be exhausted by the time she got home.

"Did you do your homework?" I asked after she rolled in late one night.

"Sure," she said, not paying me much attention.

"When?" I asked. "If every night you're up there for the play?"

At the time, drama created . . . well, drama between us, as well as the other aspects of teenage life. In fact, the conflict had gotten so intractable that I finally had gone to God in my exasperation. When she turned eighteen, I had a talk with him one evening at church. "God, you gave her to me for eighteen years to raise. Thank you for that. Now, I'm giving her back to you. I hope I've done my job."

I wasn't giving up on her, but it marked a transition for me. She was an adult who would need to be making adult decisions even though she was still living in our house. For example, one of our rules was that we wanted her to text us when she got in the car and started home at night. When Andy was out of town, she wouldn't do that no matter how much he emphasized that this requirement didn't wane just because he wasn't home. Her lack of compliance irritated Andy, because he still saw her as his teenage daughter. In my mind she'd transitioned into adult, and—after my chat with God—I decided to start letting things like this go.

That night we heard many stories. One young man said, "I just have to let you know that Ann was such a light in my life."

Listening to these words made me realize that life isn't about getting good grades, coming home on time, and following all the rules. Though those things are important, it was much more gratifying to hear that she was a young woman with friends she really loved.

"Helpful."

"Compassionate."

Being able to see my daughter through the eyes of her friends was truly an honor. And so, I quit trying to hold so tightly to the moment and let their words—their ephemeral words—apply a much needed balm to my broken heart.

"Kind," a student said as she lit a candle and smiled at us.

"Generous," said another.

"Love."

CHAPTER 10

One heart. One mind. One body.

That's the best way to describe how Andy and I related to each other during this tragedy. Our reactions and decisions were in sync, even though we were rarely alone amid the whirlwind of people and advisors and consultants and friends and church members and doctors and surgeons. Remarkably, every morning we would wake up at the same time—five o'clock—as though God knew it was necessary for us to be united even in wakefulness to face the day. During this tragedy, there was never a point where we disagreed on anything—small or big. We agreed on the details of the service, we agreed on the fact that we always needed smoothies, and we agreed on our response to the McBrides.

When Andy brought Michael into the room the evening of the shooting, I didn't stand up and yell: "Get that man out of here!" I'd already been trying to live a life of forgiveness, so I was spiritually prepared to embrace him as Andy had. That's God working through a marriage, as we navigated a very treacherous new terrain. I was proud of the way we stuck together as a team.

We came home after the funeral, boosted by the prayers of our friends and loved ones. We had food everywhere. Casseroles, hams, chocolate chip cookies, potpies, hams. Did I mention hams? People's desire to "do" for us didn't fade once the service was over. And so, we ate as much as we could, we said prayers of thankfulness over each meal, and basked in the love of our congregation.

Yet, when we were at home, in the quiet of the night without visitors or spiritual challenges or a teenager rushing through the kitchen in search of food, things were different. We sat on the couch, where we'd sat a million times before, and it felt as though we were sitting in other people's lives. Our context had changed. We'd changed.

One evening Andy reached out and placed his hand on my knee, and something happened that was a good indication of how far our lives had drifted from normal.

I recoiled.

"What's wrong?" he asked.

"I'm just not ready," I said. And it was true. Though I wasn't sure why, I wasn't interested in being romantic, in connecting with my husband the way that spouses are supposed to connect. I could tell it hurt Andy, who was reeling from the greatest tragedy we'd ever experienced. Sex is supposed to unite a couple in a way that transcends the troubles of the day, but I couldn't even let his hand rest on my knee.

"Did you know that 80 to 90 percent of marriages won't survive a child's death?" our friend Kay said to me.

"Really?" I asked in disbelief. In actuality, there are no reliable statistics on the phenomenon, but it's obvious that the added stress of a child's death is maritally challenging. I began to hear this sentiment so frequently that divorce seemed unavoidable.

And we hadn't buried just one child. We'd buried three. I'm not sure why we suffered through two stillbirths—Caitlin and Lucien—and then the death of Ann. But I knew our marriage had already been forced to weather some storms. I grieved over the babies in ways different from Andy. I'd carried them in my body, and felt a tremendous loss over their deaths. Andy, on the other hand, struggled to feel connected to these little people. It was hard to attach feelings to them because they didn't seem "real" to him.

When we attended The Compassionate Friends, things changed. Andy began to understand my grieving process, how it had affected me. I began to see that there was life after a death in the family. I didn't think I could live after Caitlin died, until I saw other people in the same circumstance living and even thriving. One of our new friends from the support group—after a very emotional session—summed it up pretty nicely: "I always think there are questions I'm going to ask God when I see him," she said. "But I have a feeling that when I see God none of those questions are going to matter anymore."

When Lucien died, I was more prepared for the experience. I knew I'd live through it, I knew Andy would grieve differently, and I knew how to process my feelings. But after Ann's death, I couldn't quite predict or mitigate the various ways loss reared its head.

After having gone through so much tragedy with grace and peace, we suddenly had problems connecting. Because we've had difficult places in our marriage before, we recognized when we were getting close to that precarious place of serious marriage issues. Ann died on April 2. By mid-April, we were no longer "close." We were in "that place."

One day I was going through the mail and dropped all the cards into a cardboard box, our receptacle for the letters and cards of sympathy that kept pouring in. We would open them, quickly read through them, and promise ourselves to go back later and soak in the love.

My leave time from work was running out. I had scheduled

myself to return on a Friday for just a few hours so I would then have the weekend off again. As the date approached, I suggested to Andy we leave town for a few days.

"What do you think about a midweek trip to Callaway Gardens?" I suggested. This retreat center is located in the southernmost foothills of the Appalachian Mountains, a quiet place for solitude and reconnecting. Our friends Joe and Cindy had gone up there for their anniversary, and they'd had a great time.

"Sure. We can take the cards and letters and take all the time we need to read them while we're there," he said.

We packed up the car, headed to the mountains, and breathed in the fresh air. I loved being away from our home and away from Tallahassee. We went to a Birds of Prey program, which was meaningful because Ann loved these big birds so much. In fact, every time I see a hawk, I think of her. There, falcons, eagles, and hawks—which couldn't be released into the wild due to injury— gave us a show, swooping right over our heads, dazzling us with their plumage, their quickness. The birds' caretakers, who wore large, protective gloves, would hold out their arms for the birds to land on them. I could totally imagine Ann, with her love of animals, being a caretaker for these damaged birds. Occasionally I'd have to look away from the show and gather myself.

Each day there, we sat in one of the garden areas with our box of cards in front of us. The gardens were an explosion of color with daffodils, tulips, and azaleas. God's love for the planet—with the vibrant, lively colors dotting the landscape—was obvious. But just as obvious was our church's love for us. There were hundreds and hundreds of kind, handwritten letters or cards with notes written lovingly in the margins. Once again, we were enveloped by the affection of our community.

We spent most of our time outside enjoying God's creation at Callaway Gardens. One afternoon I was sitting at the top of a hill looking down onto some of the formal gardens, soaking in the warm sun. When my phone rang, it jolted me back to reality.

"Kate?" It was Bob Blythe, the director of my handbell choir. "Do you have a minute?"

It was as if my community in Tallahassee was reaching across the miles to me even in that secluded place. He didn't realize we were out of town, but I didn't consider it an intrusion. It reminded me of the passage in the epistle to the Romans that says, "Neither death nor life, neither angels nor demons, neither the present nor the future, nor any powers, neither height nor depth, nor anything else in all creation, will be able to separate us from the love of God that is in Christ Jesus our Lord" (Rom. 8:38–39).

"The bell choir has been talking among ourselves, and we want to do something for Ann," he said. "We wanted to surprise you by having a song written for her. We thought of Valerie Stephenson, since she was just here for our workshop, but then she insisted she talk to you first about Ann, her personality, her life. So . . . surprise!"

Many handbell songs are dedicated to someone—a previous director of the choir, or someone who passed away. This gesture was such an honor.

I would also add that nothing can separate us from the love of the good folks at Good Shepherd. When I ended the call, I sat on the hill and felt—honestly, deeply—loved. But while I was feeling loved by the church, Andy and I still were having problems.

On the last night of the trip, when it was time to go to bed, I started feeling anxious. Under normal conditions, it would've been a perfect setting for a loving connection between spouses. I'm sure Andy couldn't help but wonder if getting me away from our now empty home would allow me to be more receptive to intimacy. This was our main area of struggle since Ann's death. Ever since, the very thought of intimacy made me brace myself, stiffen . . . not exactly the most romantic posture. That night I tried. I really did. We kissed. We touched. We got close. But then, at the moment of connection, I burst into tears.

"What's wrong with you?" Andy asked, watching me absolutely sob. "With us?"

Intimate moments are not the best time to have a discussion about intimacy. Both of us were so raw, so deeply vulnerable that it really felt more like a lament. We were already so bruised, so broken. Andy felt rejection; I felt pressure. Adding insecurity to what we'd been through was simply unbearable.

"We need to talk to somebody about this," Andy said. "We need to see someone."

As soon as we got back to Tallahassee, I made an appointment with Kay, a friend and marriage counselor who knew Ann, knew Andy and me, and knew what we'd been going through. She's an honest, wise woman, which made Andy agree to this selection. Deep down, however, I figured she'd understand my feelings because she was a woman. I was counting on her siding with me.

"I'm here to preserve your marriage," she began. "I'm here to help you keep your marriage intact as you go through this challenging time. All right. Who'd like to explain to me what's going on?"

"It's actually very, very basic," I said, in my attempt to explain the underlying issues. "Sex is tied to reproduction." She looked at me, encouraging me to go on. "I know other people want to separate the two. Sex and babies aren't tied together in their minds or experience."

Even though I had two amazing daughters, I felt as though the title of "mother" should be stripped from me. I didn't deserve it any longer because moms protect their children. With Ann's death I felt my motherhood was taken away.

"Of course, sex is so much more than reproduction," I admitted. But in that moment, when Andy and I tried to connect, it was so tightly tied to maternity that I couldn't shake the thought: *This is how we got babies. This is how this whole saga began.*

It was really that basic.

Kissing. Touching. Love. Sex. Pregnancy. Babies. Death. Failure.

Anguish is not a powerful aphrodisiac. In those moments, those unguarded moments of vulnerability, I couldn't stop it from creeping in. "It has nothing to do with Andy or my love for him."

As she listened to me explain my feelings, she nodded with compassion and understanding.

Andy explained his side as well, expressing his frustration over not being able to connect with me at a time when intimacy was of the utmost importance. "I love you," he said to me. "I just want to be with you . . . and I want you to want to be with me. I don't want you just to comply. I don't want reluctant cooperation."

"Andy, whatever it is," Kay said, "you have to accept what Kate is willing to give you. She'll come back. Just respect her during this time. You have to understand how personal this is for Kate, and give her space to recover."

I knew Kay—as a woman—would understand. In fact, her anticipated sympathy with my point of view was one of the reasons I suggested we use her.

"But Kate, you have to make the effort to be there for Andy," she said pointedly. "No matter what you feel." It took me aback a bit. She was assigning responsibility to me? "You have to work through it. You can't let yourself stay in this place. You have to realize that this is important for Andy, and it's important for your marriage."

I sat silently as she spoke directly to me.

"Andy has made the commitment to be faithful to you," she said. "To you and you alone. That's a big responsibility for him and you. You need to respect his commitment to you and honor that. As much as possible, be present for him and work toward building this very important part of your relationship back up.

"Your sex life isn't about you, and it's not about Andy," she said. "It's about your marriage and your life together."

We left counseling very sobered. After that day, Andy became more accepting of my emotional situation. Somehow, that acceptance took the pressure off and gave me the chance to open up more to Andy.

Kay had told us from the beginning that she was trying to preserve our marriage, and that's exactly what she did. Had she said what I thought she would say—something like, "Andy, you've just got to let her work through this and don't bother her and let her come back when it's time for her to come back"—who knows what would have happened?

I may have never come back.

❦

I picked up my two handbells—F and G—and positioned myself in the choir.

I love the moments right before we start practice, when people rush into the room and pick up their handbells, possibly a little frazzled by the activities of the day. No matter how frenzied life is, however, we soon find ourselves involved in an intricate mix of sound. There's something powerful about chiming in on cue, and it's easy to get wrapped up in the heavenly sounds. The harmonies twist from major to minor chords, and the songs change from one emotion to another. I love wrapping my note into the final chord. Even if I don't play the final note, I often "fake ring" by making the motion without the sound in order to participate in the experience. Sometimes I catch myself holding my breath as the final sounds dissipate into the room, which always feels a little different than when we found it.

When I got back from Callaway Gardens, I'd called Valerie

Stephenson, the arranger, author, conductor, clinician, and composer who had agreed to do the song. We discussed various songs she might be able to use. We decided she would do an arrangement of an existing song, "The Ashgrove," rather than a new composition. The handbell choir had been such a part of my life for so many years, it was very poignant that they took the time and creativity to honor my family in this way. "In order for it to be officially dedicated," she had told me, "it has to be performed in public."

We asked Good Shepherd if we could have a public presentation of the song—something simple, maybe just a prelude or reflection. When the parish found out about our handbell song for Ann, the men's choir and the children's choir wanted in on the action. Instead of a simple "performance," it became a full-blown memorial concert. We scheduled it for a crisp fall night in November. While we were practicing the song for the concert, Deb, one of the ringers, said, "Kate, I never realized that you played the last note in the song."

"Yes," I said. "I also play the first."

When Valerie had selected the music, she had no knowledge of what notes people played. The song began and ended with the G5 chime. One of my notes.

"The song that honors my daughter begins and ends with my hand," I mused.

We all stood and pondered God's goodness and his poetic, melodic arrangement of the details of our lives.

CHAPTER 11

I assume he'll spend the rest of his life in prison, right?" I asked
Helene Potlock, the Victim Assistance Program Director at the
state attorney's office.

Florida has tough crime laws, dubbed "10–20–Life." That means
that anyone who uses a gun while committing a crime will be sentenced to ten years; anyone who fires a gun while committing a
crime will be sentenced to twenty years; and anyone who injures
or kills someone with a gun will get twenty-five years to life. To
help citizens remember, the Department of Corrections sums it
up like this: "Pull a Gun—Mandatory 10 Years. Pull the Trigger—
Mandatory 20 Years. Shoot Someone—25 Years to Life (whether
they live or die)."[1] We knew Conor was going to be spending the
rest of his life in prison. It was a warm Friday in May, and we
were at the state attorney's office to discuss their strategy regarding Conor. We were waiting for the assistant state attorney, Jack
Campbell, to arrive.

"No, 10–20–Life only applies if it goes to trial and he's found
guilty. Then the judge must follow the mandatory sentencing guidelines," Helene explained. "But if it does not go to trial, the judge
does not have to follow the mandatory sentencing guidelines."

That didn't mean much to me at the moment, but I tucked it away in my mind. Jack Campbell came in, introduced himself, sat down at his desk, and placed a large file there. When he looked up at us, my recognition was immediate. This was the son of Larry Campbell, our county sheriff, who ran the jail where Conor remained incarcerated.

"The first thing I want to tell you is that the death penalty is off the table," he said. Andy and I sat across the desk from Jack, while the victim's advocate, Helene, sat in a chair to the side. "But from what I've heard, you wouldn't want to pursue that anyway."

"You're right," Andy said. "We wouldn't." If you had asked me ten years ago what my thoughts on the death penalty were, I might have said, "An eye for an eye." Over the years, I had begun to accept the Church's teaching that all life is precious from conception to natural death. We live in a country that has the means to keep dangerous criminals away from the public, so we do not need capital punishment. I don't think Jack encountered many moral or philosophical discussions of the death penalty, though. I think he was used to hearing loved ones protest that the offender *wasn't* facing the death penalty. Isn't the normal reaction one of vengeance and retribution? We even had people who offered to "take care of Conor" for us.

The death penalty in Florida is reserved for capital offenses that include first-degree murder and felony murder. First-degree murder is the most serious homicide charge, because it involves premeditation. Conor would have needed a plan to carry out the homicide in order to be charged this way. In fact, Jack argued that even if Conor thought for a second that he wanted to shoot Ann, it would have been classified as first-degree. A felony murder is when someone commits homicide during the commission of a felony (for example, a burglary) . . . sort of a "felony on top of a felony." I was relieved to hear these options were off the table.

"I just want to let you know that I will handle everything. You don't have to worry. We'll try not to go to trial," he said. "If we do go to trial, we'll try not to have you testify. We don't want you in the room. We'll spare you as much as we can." I got the feeling he'd done this a million times, and he was trying to assure us that we didn't have to participate in the process for justice to be done. In a way his confidence was reassuring. "I'll represent Ann," he continued. "I'll be her advocate."

Andy, who sat on my left, repositioned himself in his chair. I glanced over at him and noticed he'd become very still. A statue. He later told me he felt as though Jack was trying to take his fatherhood away. Ever since Ann was born, he had been her advocate and caretaker. In her death Andy was not going to relinquish his last real act of advocacy. He would always be her father, and this man could not take that away from him.

"How much time do you think he's going to spend in prison?" I asked. "Twenty-five to life?"

"I have a lot of leeway in what he's charged with," Jack said, leaning back in his chair.

"Really?" I asked. "Doesn't 10–20–Life pretty much settle it?"

"No . . . I could charge him with manslaughter and recommend five years," he said, emphasizing the words "five years" to show how preposterously short that would be—a verbal flourish to demonstrate his power in this process.

I sat straight up. "What?"

"Oh no, I wouldn't do that in this case," he said, trying to assuage me. He probably assumed I'd been offended at how little time he could spend in jail. "I *could*, but I'm not going to."

"But you could, right?" I said, leaning forward in my chair. "You *could* charge him with manslaughter, and he'd only get five years?"

Suddenly, he understood that a shorter sentence had piqued my interest, not upset me.

"We're not talking about that in this case," he backpedaled. "I mean, that's not going to happen."

He quickly focused the rest of the meeting on procedures. He explained that it could take nine months to a year to see if we would go to trial, and that they were in the process of gathering evidence.

"The defense will portray your daughter in a negative light and will portray Conor in a positive light," he said.

"But he turned himself in," I said. "He's admitted to shooting her."

"Yes, but a trial will bring everything out," he said. "No matter how Conor feels now, his defense attorney will do whatever is necessary to get him the best sentencing."

Is this one big game? I thought. The way he described it, we, the McBrides, and Conor were just pawns on a chessboard. Even if Conor didn't want to assassinate Ann's character, Jack assured us that basically the defense attorney would do it anyway. I didn't want to relive all the pain and drama of Ann's death, especially with a professional defense team aiming to tear down Ann's good name.

"I don't want that," I said. The room grew quiet as we thought about Conor's sentencing.

"Do you think any of us here in this room have been as angry as Conor was when he shot Ann?" Jack asked.

"Oh no," I said immediately. "I don't think any of us have."

"Definitely not," Andy said.

Jack paused a moment and announced, "I guarantee every one of us has been as angry as Conor."

"Well," I said, "if we're being honest, then I have been as angry as Conor." My mind returned to my dating years, when I tried to run over poor Jake McFarland with my moped. When Jake angered me outside that pizza parlor, I put the pedal to the metal. Of course, he had a chance to simply get out of the way. But what if I'd startled him? What if he'd fallen and hit his head? Then my angry flare-up would look different. A lot more serious.

"What I'm trying to say is this," Jack said. "We've all been that angry, but not one of us has picked up a gun and shot the person closest to us."

Of course, Jack's point was made: Conor was different from us civilized folks.

"And," he added, "Conor didn't call 911. He got in his car, drove around town, and then turned himself in. If this were truly an accident, he wouldn't have been afraid to call 911."

"But here's a boy who's barely nineteen years old, and he's just fired a shotgun at the head of the person he'd wanted to marry. He'd just done—and witnessed—a really horrific thing. He thought he had killed her right then," I said. Until Jack Campbell talked about it, I hadn't really thought about why Conor didn't call for help. "Shooting someone is a very physically violent thing."

"Yes, that's what I'm pointing out," Jack said. "He's done a very violent thing."

"But you expect him to just call 911 and say, 'I shot my girl-friend'?" I asked. "I can forgive him for being so shocked at what happened that he did not immediately pick up the phone. He contemplated killing himself, so he must have been extremely upset and disturbed by what he'd just done."

"I know you've forgiven Conor," Jack said to me. "And forgive-ness is good. I, too, am a Christian. But . . ."

As he let his sentence hang unfinished in the air, I knew exactly what he meant. Forgiveness is generally a good thing, but there are limits. Everyone knows that.

That night I lay down on my side of the bed and listened as Andy's breathing changed into the cadence of sleep. I pulled the covers up to my neck and relived the conversation with Jack Campbell. It's one thing to think that Conor was going to have to spend the rest of his life in prison because the law demanded it. It's quite another to realize that he doesn't actually have to spend the rest of his life in prison. When Jack told me about the discretion he had over the charge, it was another moment of conviction. What were we willing to do? What were we going to do now that we could make a difference?

"I, too, am a Christian. But . . ."

There was a lot packed into that last syllable. It somehow quantified forgiveness, limited it, made it seem a tad unreasonable. People have described our actions to Conor as "radical forgiveness," but we thought of it as basic Christianity. Were we doing anything more radical than what Christ did on the cross? "Father, forgive them, for they do not know what they are doing," he'd said (Luke 23:34).

Yet, as I contemplated it, I got it. In some ways it was easier to forgive Conor, knowing that the state was *not* going to forgive him and that he'd be locked up forever. But how far was I willing to take my forgiveness now that I knew there were other options? Were we willing to step in or just sit back and let the system go forward? I suddenly felt responsible for what would happen to Conor.

Did we really want him to spend twenty-five years to life in prison?

I turned over on my side and could see the clock: 2:37 a.m.

CHAPTER 12

$\mathcal{W}$hen Andy was in the process of becoming a deacon, he was assigned a wonderful mentor named Marcus Hepburn. As the emergency manager for the Florida Catholic Conference, Marcus coordinated the state's seven Catholic dioceses for disaster response and trained rural volunteers to respond effectively during tornadoes, hurricanes, and droughts. His wife, Toni, managed a Ronald McDonald House; and Marcus was a president of the Big Bend Homeless Coalition, a member of Tallahassee Equality Action Ministry (which works on social-justice issues), and an activist in prison ministry. In fact, Governor Jeb Bush gave him a Point of Light Award for social and religious activism in 2004.

"Marcus, what do you know about Wakulla prison?" Andy asked him one day. "Do you think Conor could get in there once he's sentenced?" We were concerned a regular state prison would not be the best place for Conor and were investigating whether or not we could get him into a faith-based prison. It could only be good for him to be surrounded by people of faith.

"Wakulla Correctional Institution is one of the faith- and character-based residential programs in state," he said, referring to the facility located just south of Tallahassee. "They offer faith-based programming to inmates to improve their lives so they don't just sit in jail for years." The program had fewer correctional issues among the inmates and attempted to reduce recidivism by teaching the prisoners life skills.

"That sounds perfect," Andy said. He had been visiting with Conor because Andy did not want him to sink into despair or hopelessness. He knew that self-forgiveness would be impossible without God. "Or as perfect as being in jail can be," he said.

"I know an Episcopal priest named Allison DeFoor, and his assignment is Wakulla prison," he said. "Do you want me to introduce you?"

"Wait—*his* assignment?"

"Yes, he's a man named Allison," Marcus laughed. "You have to speak to him."

∽

It had been two months since Ann died.

On Memorial Day weekend we accepted a dinner invitation from Jerry and Margaret Haynes. Jerry was also a deacon at Good Shepherd church. We'd had a little time to adjust to our "new normal" of life without our daughter. In the middle of dinner, Jerry's phone rang and he excused himself to answer it. I could tell by his tone of voice that something was wrong. When he came back into the room, our fears were confirmed.

"Marcus was moving a mattress in his garage," he said. "He fell backward and hit his head and is in really bad shape."

"Where is he?" I asked.

"The Neuro ICU at Tallahassee Memorial," he said.

This, of course, was exactly where Ann was treated.

We all quickly finished our dinner and drove to the hospital.

"How do you think you'll feel going back to the hospital?" Andy asked as we rushed to see Marcus.

"At least we'll know our way around," I said.

And I was surprised at how relatively easy it was to go back into that place. For some, I can imagine there would be the anxiety of, "I can't go in. I don't want to open that door. I don't want to walk down that hallway." But once I'd forgiven Conor, I didn't hold all that anxiety any longer. Marcus's room was directly across the hall from Ann's. In fact, we exchanged awkward glances with one of the nurses who had taken care of Ann just eight weeks prior. *Wait, I know you, but didn't you already leave?* I made a mental note to catch her on the way out.

"I'm so sorry," I said as I hugged his wife, Toni. As we stood next to Marcus's bed, suddenly the roles were reversed. Andy and I were the ones comforting instead of the ones receiving comfort. As we talked to Toni, a man came into the room. He had salt-and-pepper hair framing his dark eyes, and he wore a beard.

"Hey, big guy," he said to Marcus, who was unconscious. The man was shorter than I was, but his personality seemed to take up the whole room. As we talked to Toni, Marcus would do things that indicated he was still in there somewhere; he moved and opened his eyes, so it looked as though he might have a chance of recovery. But Marcus was on blood thinners for his heart, and they weren't able stop his internal bleeding. Within a week, he would die of his injuries.

As we waited, Toni said, "Allison, would you mind praying?"

A man named Allison? That's when it dawned on us. This was the man with whom Marcus promised to connect us, a promise he kept in a most terrible way. As we left, Andy grabbed Allison in the corridor. "I'm Andy Grosmaire. Marcus said you were the one I need to talk to because I have some questions about helping someone get into Wakulla prison."

"That'll be tough because I don't really have any influence over that," he said. "But here's my card. Give me a call and we'll talk about it."

A few days later, Andy and I went to downtown Tallahassee to Allison's office. It was located in an old redbrick building with a clock tower on one corner, and the inside looked like a movie set for "old Southern lawyer." The staircase and the floors were crafted from dark, worn wood, and the accents were made of brass. We waited for him to arrive in his small office, which was tucked in the upstairs corner.

Had Allison shown up matching his stately law office, he would've appeared in a seersucker suit and a bow tie. In fact, his family has been in Florida for seven generations—a rarity, especially in this part of Florida. Before becoming an Episcopal priest, he was a judge and the sheriff of Monroe County, a public defender, a prosecutor, Republican Governor Bob Martinez's running mate nominee for lieutenant governor in 1990, and Governor Jeb Bush's "Everglades Czar." He came to the ministry later in life, when he traded his political aspirations for spiritual ones. Though he's been known to wear bow ties, he showed up that day in a Hawaiian shirt, shorts, and sandals.

"Hey guys, come on in and sit down," he said. "Push those papers off the desk. How can I help you?"

Andy and I told him our story. "The grand jury came back and has charged him with first-degree murder, so we just know he's going to prison for life. It'd be great if he would be able to go to Wakulla."

"Sadly, there's not a lot I can do about getting Conor into Wakulla, because there's a waiting list that's two or three years long. It's a very popular place because there's much less violence and a lot of accountability," Allison said. "It sounds like what you really want is restorative justice."

"Restorative what?" Andy said.

"Aren't you Catholic?"

"Yes," Andy said, taken aback by the question.

"Then why aren't you pursuing restorative justice? That's what Catholics are all about, right?"

"Restorative justice," he repeated as we stared at him blankly. "Google it."

And with those two words—*Google it*—our trajectory with Conor changed forever.

At the time, Andy was taking a class on Catholic moral theology and was assigned a term paper. The more he studied restorative justice, the more it intrigued him. When his professor told him that he could write his term paper on it, instead of the other listed topics, Andy began researching it more intensely.

One afternoon I was washing clothes in the laundry room when he came in.

"Kate, this restorative justice is really incredible," he said excitedly, holding a book called *The Little Book of Restorative Justice* by Howard Zehr. He held it as if he'd just found buried treasure in the backyard and couldn't wait to show me.

"What is it, exactly?" I asked.

"It's just common sense," he said, before plunging into his explanation. "Basically, when someone has committed a crime, he needs to acknowledge the wrongdoing. The victims need to grieve their losses, tell their story, have their questions answered, and have their needs addressed. The offender needs to accept responsibility for his actions and try to repair the damage if possible."

Zehr says restorative justice is based on three principles:

1. Crime is the violation of people and of interpersonal relationships.
2. Violations create obligations on the part of the offender.

3. The central obligation is to right the wrongs.

"Basically, it's based on the idea that everyone is connected," he said, "and crime rips that connectivity in a way that needs to be addressed." Though Zehr's first principle addresses the relational aspect of crime, the criminal justice system does not prioritize this relationship. The system doesn't really meet the needs of victims, because it wasn't designed to do so. The definition of "crime" doesn't even include victims. Rather, a crime is something done to harm the state. This, of course, is what Andy reacted to in Jack Campbell's office, when Jack said he'd handle everything and be Ann's advocate. The state stands in for the victim, which leaves the victim out of a process that so profoundly affected his or her life. In Ann's case, it ended hers.

Restorative justice aims to meet some of the needs of crime victims, such as providing real information about what happened. In our current system of justice, we ask: What law was broken? Who broke it? How should they be punished? Restorative justice asks a different set of questions: Who was harmed? What do they need? Whose obligation is it to meet those needs?

Frequently, victims never truly understand what happened during the crime. Because they are so separated from the criminal justice process, they only hear—sometimes from their seats in the courthouse—partial truths spun to help defend the perpetrator. Because it's not usually possible to get true details from a trial, restorative justice allows victims (or their advocates) to speak directly to the criminal.

Next, restorative justice allows the victim to tell his or her story, in what is hopefully a healing and transformative way. Crime disrupts the victims' views of themselves, their life stories, and the way the world operates. To be able to get beyond the horrific crimes, victims must "re-story" the incident by telling the story in significant ways. Sometimes it's also critical for the criminal to understand the effect his or her actions had on the victim's life. This empowers the victim in a way that the criminal justice system—not designed to include the victim—cannot do.

Lastly, restorative justice gives the criminal the opportunity to make restitution. Sometimes it's vindicating for a criminal to try to make up for what was lost.

"But what if it's not possible to replace what was taken?" I asked.

"This book addresses that," he said, before flipping through the pages and reading me a story about an elderly woman who had been robbed of her wedding ring and jewelry. She chose to sit down with the young man who had stolen the jewelry to explain how her jewelry had been a family heirloom of enormous sentimental importance. Once the man who'd stolen it—for the money—heard her story, he better understood that he'd taken more than a ring from this woman. "In other words, restorative justice encourages offenders to understand the consequences of what they've done and to empathize with the people they've harmed."

Which, as I thought about it, was true. The adversarial way that the system is set up discourages people from even admitting that they've done anything wrong at all. Conor had already pled not guilty in court, though he had confessed when he walked into the police station. Offenders rarely have an opportunity to make it up to their victims. Even when people are punished, they're never actually held accountable for their crimes. The restorative justice Andy was telling me about attempts to hold the criminal accountable in ways that benefit the victim, the criminal, and the community.

"In fact, restorative justice factors in the community in ways that the criminal justice system can't," he said. I poured some detergent into the washer while Andy turned a page in the book.

"Communities are considered 'secondary victims,' because they're impacted by crime as well."

"But is it possible to use it when there's more to restore than some jewelry?" Of course I was thinking of Ann, but I didn't want to say it. While I wanted the best for Conor, his path was already determined: life in prison. Still, part of me was curious if restorative justice could be used in a case as challenging as ours.

Andy read to me a story about a young woman whose father was murdered, and she participated in a victim/offender dialogue with his killer before he was released back into the community. Though this book emphasized that forgiveness was not a necessary part of restorative justice, it certainly gave forgiveness more of a fighting chance. In this story the young lady forgave her father's murderer.

"You just don't hear of things like this," I said, matching some socks. For some reason, Andy's black socks all seemed to be of different varieties. I briefly considered matching a pair that were both black but had different patterns. "Forgiveness is such a foreign concept. Do you think restorative justice could really work?"

CHAPTER 13

*A*ndy looked across the table at Michael McBride, who took a sip of espresso. They had already ordered their food, and were waiting for it to be delivered to the table. Andy reached up to their order number and rearranged it in the metal stand.

There was almost nothing to say. There was almost too much to say.

After one man's son killed the other's daughter, it would have been easy for the men to hash it out, over and over, examining every detail for missed clues. It would have been natural for accusations to fly, for excuses to be made, for anger to be shown. But even though there was a lot that could have been said, sometimes it was hard to say anything at all. Their conversations were heartfelt and personal. It was hard for anyone to believe that the two met every Friday for lunch, but this unusual pair shared a common, tragic bond: both had lost a child in a very significant, dramatic way. Andy had lost Ann to death. Forever. Michael had lost Conor to prison, possibly for life.

"So, I've been reading about this concept called restorative justice," Andy said as he poured sweetener into his iced tea and swirled his spoon around in his glass.

"What is that?" Michael asked, his eyebrow raised in a parenthesis of curiosity. "Julie hasn't been sleeping because she can't stand the thought of Conor spending his entire life in jail. She tosses all night."

Andy explained restorative justice in as much detail as he knew. "The good thing about it is that Kate and I would have a say in the length of Conor's sentence. The 'restorative justice circle' allows everyone to come to an agreement on what the sentence should be."

"Do you think it could work for Conor?" Michael asked. At this, the waitress appeared with their food and left it at the table.

"I'm not sure. In order to start the process, we need a restorative justice facilitator, and I'm not sure where to start looking," Andy said, pulling his food to him and picking up his sandwich. "There's nothing like it here in Leon County. Then we will have to convince Jack Campbell to agree to it."

"What if it wasn't just us asking?" Michael said. "What if we got a petition and circulated it among our friends?"

Andy thought about this idea. "It definitely couldn't hurt," he said before biting into his meal.

Later, Michael told his wife about all he and Andy had discussed. Without hesitation, Julie latched onto the concept like a drowning person to a life preserver. With the help of Julie, Andy began trying to figure out if restorative justice could be implemented in Conor's case. They joined chat groups and forums. They called and e-mailed restorative justice experts, most of whom never bothered to respond. The two or three who did bother all had bad news.

"Sorry, but there's no one in the state of Florida who can do this for you," one e-mail read.

Andy actually talked to one of the most prominent restorative justice experts in the country who echoed the sentiment. "I can't help you with this." No reason was given.

After months of effort, Andy got a call from Julie.

"I found someone," she said. "Her name is Sujatha Baliga and she works in Oakland, California. She gave me her phone number and wants to talk to you and Kate."

What Julie didn't tell us was that she had found Sujatha by way of Howard Zehr, "the grandfather of restorative justice" and author of the book Andy read aloud to me in the laundry room. Basically, she decided she would not give up until she talked to him. "Hi, my name is Julie McBride. My son shot and killed his fiancée, and her parents are interested in doing restorative justice," she said when she got him on the telephone.

"Mm-hmm," he said. "You don't need just a restorative justice practitioner. You need a restorative justice lawyer. Let me make some calls."

Howard called Sujatha, who worked for the National Council on Crime and Delinquency in Oakland, California. She had been working in Alameda County to establish a restorative justice youth program in the juvenile justice system there. When she got a call from Howard, she immediately rejected the idea.

"No way, Howard," she said. "You were talking to the mother of the young man who committed this crime. Of course she wants to pursue this."

"I know you believe restorative justice could apply in cases like this."

"Of course I do. But how could we pull it off in a capital case in Florida?" Sujatha asked. "No chance, Howard."

Howard, who is a laid-back, peaceful Mennonite, finally agreed. "Okay, but you talk to her and tell her why it's not going to work. She needs a lawyer's perspective—someone who understands how restorative justice works within the legal system."

"Go ahead and give her my number. But I don't have anything good to tell her. What I do here with kids in California is never going to happen in a capital case in a Southern state."

Within the hour Sujatha received a call from Julie, whom she found to be warm, grateful, and serious about helping her son. Through her tears, Julie described what happened that horrible Sunday: how Conor planned to take his own life, but took Ann's instead, how he turned himself in, how he confessed. "Everyone wants to use restorative justice in this case," she concluded.

"I'm sorry, but this is a capital crime in Florida," Sujatha said. "Even if the parents of the victim wanted to pursue restorative justice, it takes eighteen months to get a process like this started."

"Actually, the Grosmaires introduced us to the concept," Julie said.

"Wait, the parents of the victim?" Sujatha asked.

"Yes! They're the ones who told us about restorative justice."

"You're in contact with them?"

"Frequently," she said. "In fact, they regularly visit Conor in jail, and my husband meets with Ann's dad every week. I just went to breakfast with them on Saturday."

Sujatha paused on the other end of the line. "I have to say, it sounds like a remarkable situation. But I'm just not sure what we can do in a first-degree homicide case at this stage of the game."

Julie began to cry. "Won't you let me just hire you to see what you can do?"

"In Oakland I facilitate restorative practices to keep children out of the juvenile justice system," Sujatha said, very kindly. "You know, for crimes like burglary and robbery, or teen-dating violence." She explained how she gathered families, victims, law enforcement, the state attorney, and community members for in-person meetings with the juvenile who committed the crime. Then they agree on a plan for how to deal with the offense in a way that benefits all involved. "But I've never used restorative justice for a homicide case with gun charges," she said. "Especially not for first-degree murder."

"I know you can't promise anything," Julie said, sniffling. She'd been trying for months to get a response from a restorative justice expert, and she felt her chance was slipping through her hands. "But please just talk with the Grosmaires."

"Even if the parents are on board, it took me years to build trust with the district attorney here. I can't imagine it working in a homicide case in the Florida panhandle. I can't work for you—in good conscience—because I don't think it will work."

"But you'll talk to them?"

Sujatha paused, trying to figure out how far this should go. She knew this wouldn't work, but she didn't want to dash the hopes of this desperate mother.

"Sure," she said, though she figured this would be the end of it. She assumed Julie was just another worried, unrealistic mother valiantly doing whatever she could to help her son. "You can give them my contact information. If they want to call me, they can."

❧

My cell phone buzzed on my desk, so I flipped it over and saw Andy's name pop up on the screen.

"Julie called and gave me the number of a lawyer in California who specializes in restorative justice," Andy said. "Do you want to call her?"

"Sure!" I said. Using the conference call feature on our iPhones, we dialed her number and were connected immediately.

"Sujatha Baliga?" I asked. "Julie McBride gave us your number. Do you have time to talk?"

"Of course," she said.

Andy and I explained our situation. We told her about Ann and Conor's tumultuous relationship, how their tragic fight ended in death, how Conor turned himself in, how his dad showed up at the hospital, how we forgave Conor, and how I visited him in jail that Friday to tell him. Then I explained Allison's suggestion that we pursue restorative justice.

"God forgives us," Andy said, "so we forgave Conor."

For a moment no one spoke. Sujatha cleared her throat, pushing away the emotion that I thought I'd detected in her voice.

"Have you met with the state attorney?" she asked.

"Yes, and the death penalty is already off the table," I said. "Andy and I don't want Conor to spend the rest of his life behind bars. What is the point of an able-bodied young man sitting in a cell every day for thirty years? Wouldn't it be better if he could spend half of his sentence in prison, but the other half working to repair the harm he's done? We know he can't give us back Ann's life—that is a debt he can never repay. But he can take his life and dedicate it to the things that she would have done—things like animal rescue. Wouldn't community service be better than just being locked away? If the case doesn't go to trial, then maybe we can make a difference in the sentence that Conor receives." I paused.

"Can you help us use the restorative justice process to handle his case?" I asked.

"It'll be an uphill battle," she said. "Restorative justice dialogues in serious cases like this happen, but only after the person who caused the harm is already into a long prison sentence, often just before he is released. The model I work with, restorative justice diversion, works because we have an arrangement with the district attorney. Here in Alameda County it's for young people who have committed crimes. The DA's office will refer cases to us that they think will work well. When the participants in the circle, including the youth, come to an agreement on what the outcome should be, the district attorney never charges the youth with the crime. There's no similar process in your jurisdiction, and even if there were, this case is too serious for the DA to agree to use it."

"Part of the reason we want to do this is to have a say in Conor's sentence. But I want answers," Andy said. "We can't get answers in the traditional criminal justice system. What were Ann's last words? What kind of argument could've possibly caused this?"

"I've worked with incarcerated people to prepare them for Victim Offender Dialogues," Sujatha said. "From the time they commit their offense, they are coached to say nothing, deny everything. People serving time often don't even speak to their cellmates about what they are in for and have espoused their innocence for so long that we have to spend a lot of time with them just to get them to admit what they did. Silence is conditioned into them."

"We know what we want to do has never been done before, but we also know that this is what God wants us to do. It's about us, but it's also about showing others that there is another way," I said.

"Okay," she said reluctantly. "Let's see what we can do then."

When she ended the phone call, I realized I'd been holding my breath when I wasn't talking. We didn't know that Sujatha had intended to break it to us gently that it was never going to work. Later she admitted that something in our voices made it impossible for her to say "no chance" as easily as she'd said it to Howard Zehr.

"I don't think she's ever met anybody like us," Andy said.

❧

Sujatha's first call was to Conor's defense attorney, Greg Cummings. After she talked to him, she immediately called us. "Okay, I have some news, but it's sort of delicate." Every time she called about something she thought would be upsetting, she spoke with great sensitivity. "In order for me to have access to all the evidence and all the materials, I'm technically going to have to be part of the defense team. I wouldn't be a traditional member of the defense team," she said. "I'd really occupy a space somewhere in the middle—including both Conor's interests and Ann's—so I can help everyone. They'll bring me on as an expert in restorative justice, but if that bothers you guys at all, then I won't do it."

"No, that's great news, right?" I asked.

"I just wanted you to know it doesn't mean I'm Conor's defense lawyer. I'm not going to defend him in any way. I'm only doing this so I can have access to information and preserve the confidentiality of the process."

"That's fine," Andy said. "We get that." And it was true. We completely trusted Sujatha, this person whom we'd never met, this attorney from the other side of the country who reluctantly got involved in our case against her better judgment.

What could go wrong?

⁂

"Do you want to publicize it in the newspaper?" my handbell director asked me a few days before the memorial concert. It was a disconcerting question. On November 14 Good Shepherd planned to hold "Joy of My Heart: A Musical Memorial" at the church. This concert had begun as a way to publicly perform the handbell song written to honor Ann, but it had grown when the Men's Choir and the Youth Chorale also decided to honor her. Three of the children in the choir even planned on playing instruments—a cello and two violins.

Because the *Tallahassee Democrat* has a religious section on Saturdays, my director wondered if we should allow them to do a story on it to raise community awareness. I wasn't so sure. We'd avoided all media up until this point because I always figured they would misquote us—an inevitability I just didn't need. I wasn't sure if more publicity for the concert was worth the probable interview request. And so, in the end, we publicized the concert and gave the reporter a copy of our talk to use for quotations.

When the night finally arrived, the sanctuary began to fill. Once again I was deeply touched by my church family's commitment to remembering Ann and loving us so well. In the foyer Michael and Julie McBride had set up a little table that had a stack of petitions that simply stated: "I agree with the Grosmaires in their pursuit of restorative justice in the case against Conor McBride."

As concertgoers came into the church, the McBrides asked them to sign this petition, which we planned to give to Jack Campbell eventually. So far they had experienced great success in getting the communities of faith to support the petition efforts. When Michael asked the pastor of First Baptist if his church would announce and support the petition, his immediate response was, "Absolutely." The people at Good Shepherd gathered around the table and formed a line to wait on the opportunity to sign the piece of paper.

This touched the McBrides, who were having trouble finding peace. Michael said he couldn't help but think distressing thoughts. He'd ask himself, *Where did I fail as a father? Why did I lose my faith? What could I have done to prevent this? Why did I not see it coming? Why did I own a gun?* Though the community gathered around him and Andy met with him regularly, Michael began to realize he needed something more.

After taking the petition to various churches—and parking lots—Julie took one to work. There, her coworkers happily signed—including the daughter of State Attorney Willie Meggs, who would later have to authorize Conor's sentence. Even though restorative justice might be unusual for our area of the country, we could at least show him that the community supported it.

It was poignant to be able to perform the handbell song

dedicated to Ann, and when the children sang a song it split me wide open. It was called "Take These Wings," and was about someone finding a dying bird on the ground. The bird gently encourages the person who found her to learn to fly, see, and sing—to really enjoy life while we have it. I'm not sure why it touched me so deeply, but something about the innocence of the children singing it combined with Ann's love of birds struck me in just the right way.

At the end of the concert, we were given some time to thank everyone. "I can't tell you how much it means to us to see so many of you coming out to honor our daughter," I said, before Andy told the story of Ann asking him from her hospital bed to forgive Conor.

"I didn't think it was possible," he said. "But we have forgiven Conor, and we would love to pursue restorative justice for him."

"Some of you may have noticed the petitions in the foyer," I said. "Please take a moment and sign them on your way out." Afterward, I noticed the line of people waiting to sign the petition snaked through the foyer.

∾

In the spring of 2011, we went to Allison DeFoor's downtown office for a meeting with Allison, Julie and Michael McBride, and Greg Cummings. Andy (who was in Fort Lauderdale) and Sujatha (who was in Oakland) participated in a conference call. It was close to a year after Ann had died.

"So, how are we going to do this?" Allison began. "How are we going to have a restorative justice process in a state that doesn't have a restorative justice process, in a county that doesn't have a state attorney set up to deal with this? How are we going to present this to the state attorney's office in a way that will make them buy into it even though they've never done it before?"

The three lawyers—Allison, Greg, and Sujatha—didn't speak for a few moments as they pondered what seemed to be an impossible situation. We needed a place where all of us could be together in the same place, but where the conversation would be considered "privileged."

"I've never practiced law in Florida," Sujatha began. "So why don't you guys begin by telling me about the Florida process? I'm just not that familiar with it."

Greg and Allison discussed the normal steps of the criminal justice system. Suddenly Allison smacked the table and exclaimed, "The pre-plea conference!"

"Right," Greg said. "That should work."

"Explain to me exactly how it works," Sujatha said.

"It's different in every state," said Allison, "but in the state of Florida, the state attorney and the defense attorney get together for a meeting called the pre-plea conference. Anybody can attend, but usually just the two attorneys meet to go through all the files. Conor could technically go, and everything he says would be confidential."

"Right," Greg added. "It's privileged, which means if Conor were to say, 'I robbed a bank that day too,' they couldn't charge him with robbing a bank. He could be free to say whatever he wanted without it affecting his case."

"And we would be there too?" Andy asked. Even though his voice came through the speaker sounding tinny, I could tell it was full of hope.

"Yes," Allison said. "Anybody can be at a pre-plea conference. That's the beauty of it."

Allison was—as Deacon Marcus had promised—a unique, unforgettable man. Andy and I have compared him to a grenade rolling into a room. Here's the idea—boom—here's the solution.

"I have to admit," Sujatha said, "it sounds like it would really work." Traditionally, no one but the defense attorney and the prosecutor would attend this meeting . . . not even the defendant. Since nothing from the meeting is admissible at trial, it was the perfect solution. We decided that Conor, the McBrides, the two attorneys, Andy, and I would attend the meeting. We talked about having a community representative. We made a note to contact the local domestic violence support group to see if it were possible to have someone from that community represented. Given our short time frame, Sujatha had concerns about how it would work to include them. In established restorative justice practices, the community representatives are trained and understand and support restorative justice. It might be difficult, if not impossible, to find someone willing to participate on such short notice.

"The next step," Sujatha said, "is for the Grosmaires to write Jack Campbell a letter asking him for this restorative justice process."

"We started a petition, actually," I said. "We have more than a thousand signatures from people in the community who were willing to say, 'I agree with the Grosmaires in their pursuit of restorative justice in the case against Conor McBride.'"

"Where'd you get them?"

"At a concert, around the community, in our neighborhood," Andy said. "We've been collecting them for months." In fact, the McBrides had done an amazing job reaching the community with our message of restorative justice. Once, when they were doing a petition drive in a parking lot, we met some Quakers who were very supportive of our effort.

"Definitely include those," Sujatha said.

"Any advice on what to say to Jack?" I asked. I realized that he was the last barrier in getting Conor's case processed this way.

"Mention that the conversation needs to be privileged, so he'll understand why we want to talk at the pre-plea conference," Greg said.

"But you don't want it to sound too lawyerly," Allison said. "He'll see through it and know we're helping you write it."

We talked for a while, framing out the contents of the letter. After we settled on language, Sujatha paused.

"Now it's up to you," she said. "You have to convince Jack Campbell to give this a chance."

CHAPTER 14

*M*y hands paused over the keyboard as I thought about what combinations of words might inspire Jack Campbell to seriously consider our request. As the Leon County assistant state attorney, he was no stranger to North Florida's high-profile murder cases. But he'd never handled a murder case this way.

"Neither has Sujatha," Andy reminded me. "Just write it. Worst he can say is no."

"No one has said no to us up to this point. If we ask reasonably, he'll have to say yes," I said.

As I sat there looking at the screen, the sheer improbability of what I was asking threatened me. *Is there a way to reasonably ask a state attorney to use restorative justice for a capital crime?* Jack Campbell had made it clear that he would take care of everything for us. He was used to driving the bus and having the victims come along for the ride. I tried to push the negative thoughts from my head. It was getting late, and I wanted to get this done before I went to sleep.

"As you know, we are interested in pursuing a course that includes restorative justice," I wrote, before continuing to explain our situation. When I got to the end, I signed it, "Sincerely, Andy and Kate Grosmaire."

The next day, Andy drove it—as well as all our petitions—to his office.

"This is for Jack Campbell," Andy said as he handed the thick packet of papers to the receptionist, who politely accepted the package and went back to her work.

Days turned into weeks. After a month with no response, Andy suggested we e-mail him.

"I don't want to annoy the man who holds Conor's future in his hands," I said.

Finally, the amount of time with no response became so unreasonable that a gentle e-mail nudge seemed appropriate. Once again we carefully composed a note to him, which we sent through Conor's attorney, Greg.

"You're not going to believe this," Greg said. "Jack never got your letter and never saw the petitions."

"What happened to them?" Andy asked. "Why do you think I drove them down to his office and hand-delivered them?"

"They misplaced them," Greg said, trying to smooth over the loss. Julie and Andy had gone to so much trouble to collect them all. Was it for nothing?

Well, we knew it was definitely not for nothing. The McBrides had been deeply affected by the signature gathering for the petition. They hadn't been churchgoers throughout their marriage. In fact, Michael had proclaimed that "there is no God" after his brother had unexpectedly passed away from a brain aneurism when Conor was a boy. As the McBrides collected signatures for the petitions, however, they saw firsthand the strength and love of a Christian community. Together, they began to search for a message of faith by attending the Good Shepherd six o'clock mass. Michael still maintained that he was not looking for religion, but he began to believe the statement of faith proclaimed each week had been written just for him.

"It'll be okay," I told Andy, placing my hand on his shoulder. "So now that we know Jack has our request, what do we do?"

"Wait for his response," Greg said.

There's a reason *wait* is a four-letter word.

To my surprise, however, I got a very brief, perfunctory e-mail from Jack later that very day.

"Contact your restorative justice expert," he wrote, "and proceed with your restorative justice circle."

CHAPTER 15

We were so excited. Jack Campbell had given Sujatha permission to contact the Leon County jail and do whatever it took to make the circle happen; to be made easier (we hoped) since the man who ran the jail, Sheriff Larry Campbell, was Jack's father.

The circle would take place at the prison itself. It was much easier to keep Conor where he was and bring the rest of us in than it was to arrange to transport him. A deputy sheriff would be right outside the room where we'd meet. All the details were falling into place.

Now that the "restorative justice circle" had been scheduled, Sujatha had to make her way from Oakland all the way to Tallahassee.

As she began making her travel arrangements, we insisted she stay with us during her visit. Although we had only spoken over the phone, we felt so close to her. She had been a true advocate for our cause. It never occurred to me that it might be seen as inappropriate, or that people would have seen this as a professional relationship with boundaries and rules that needed to be respected. Sujatha was reminded by a colleague that restorative justice is about breaking boundaries, and our case certainly fit that description. Sujatha accepted our invitation.

It was Father's Day, and I was upstairs rushing to put the finishing touches on the guest room. I often say, "I am no Martha," referring to the sister in the gospel who always made sure the meals were prepared and dishes cleaned. But I'm no Martha Stewart either. The "guest room" was nothing more than Allyson's old room, which hadn't changed much since she left for college. No coverlet and bevy of matching pillows with Anne Geddes baby portraits on the walls. A simple quilt, and one pillow. I did find a small basket that I filled with little niceties. Downstairs, I heard Andy opening the door and having a conversation. I went to the top of the stairs, where I saw Sujatha for the first time. She was short with caramel skin, dark hair streaked with silver, and dark eyes that gleamed even after her cross-country flight. Under the sparkle of her nose stud was a broad smile.

"Is it still okay that I stay here?" she asked, walking up the stairs to greet me.

Seeing her filled me with an immense sense of relief. She seemed to emanate wisdom, knowledge, and compassion. When she reached the top of the stairs, I couldn't help but embrace her. As I was in her arms, I was almost overcome by her strong, calming, maternal presence that made it seem that everything was going to work out.

As Sujatha settled in her room to take a nap after her flight, I brought up dinner plans. "Are you a vegetarian? Do you eat eggs, milk?" In all our phone conversations, the focus had been on us, our needs, and the case. Sujatha talked about her life in the context of the work that she did, but bits and pieces of her personal life peeked through. We knew she was born in America to Indian parents.

"Well, yes," she said, "but just make whatever you like. I'll find something to eat."

Thankfully, I had anticipated the possibility that she was a vegetarian and had planned dinner accordingly.

At dinner we talked about everything. She asked about Conor and what our relationship had been like in the past.

"We always liked Conor," Andy said. "In fact, he gave us quite a scare a few weeks before prom." He proceeded to tell Sujatha about the car accident he'd had about a mile from our house.

"We always said it was a miracle that God saved his life," I said. "But it's hard now . . . now that we know that he'd go on to take Ann's life. Sometimes I wonder why God didn't just let Conor die that night. Then I'd still have my daughter."

Sujatha listened compassionately, and Andy talked about how God had a plan for Conor's life, referring to Romans 8:28: "And we know that in all things God works for the good of those who love him, who have been called according to his purpose."

I concluded that "why?" is not the worst question you can ask, but it very well might be the least productive. Sometimes there's never a good answer.

We also delved more into Sujatha's background. "Are you Buddhist?"

"Yes," she answered, opening up to us. "I grew up Hindu, but with no Hindu temple in our small Pennsylvania town, I actually attended Catholic mass many Sundays with a friend of mine."

We all smiled at the "coincidence."

In our increasingly segregated society—where you rarely meet people with whom you disagree—it's not common to have so many people of different faiths pulling on the same oars.

I'm not one of those people who thinks that beliefs and theology don't matter, but our efforts in the restorative justice arena remind me of American Congregationalist theologian Lyman Abbott's words from 1893: "All truth is ours, gather it where you will . . . Yea, whosoever honestly, earnestly studies the book of

All dressed up and ready for her first Easter! Ann with Kate, 1991.

Baby Ann always had time to chill with big sister Sarah.

Ann hanging out with her "girls." She loved her Precious Moments dolls.

Allyson, Ann, and Sarah (left to right) helping Grandpa with his yardwork.

A bird lover early on, Ann poses with a parrot at Gulf World—with a little help.

From petting to offering a little food, Ann never shied away from any animal.

A Girl Scout trip to Gulf World gave Ann the opportunity to pose with her friend Brittney and tropical birds.

The girls rest with Dad after a tour of the Memphis Botanical Gardens. *Left to right: Allyson, Andy, Ann, and Sarah*

Mutiny on the Bounty: Ann and Allyson trying to turn the winch and raise the anchor.

Ann shared her love of horses with her Aunt Heather from
whom she inherited B.J. *Left to right: Ann, B.J., Andy*

(above) Ann was a natural on
whatever horse she was riding.

(left) Andy and Ann are ready to hit the
trail in the Great Smoky Mountains.

Khadijah, who hand-crocheted a beautiful afghan for Ann's graduation, and Ann enjoying feathers and friends at the Red Hills Horse Trials in Tallahassee, March 2008.

Ann and Conor, dressed up and ready for the Leon High School Prom, 2009.

Ann and Conor help out at his sister Katy's sixteenth birthday party, 2010.

Courtesy Khadijah Gray

Good Shepherd Catholic Church, our faith community.

Tallahassee Memorial Hospital, the regional trauma center where Ann was taken after she was shot on March 28.

Wakulla Correctional Institution, where Conor now resides, became a Faith- and Character-Based Institution in 2005.

Ann's oil portrait—a kind surprise, prepared by
the funeral home for Ann's service.

nature or book of history or the book of the human heart, and endeavors to find God's truth, is speaking some word that the world needs to hear; and every word of truth is a word of God. And it belongs to us."

The truth in this situation was forgiveness and justice—notions that transcend the categories that define us. That's how a couple of Catholics listened to the advice of an Episcopal priest, who led us to a Mennonite, who introduced us to a Buddhist, who worked with Protestant parents to attempt what everyone wanted: restorative justice.

Would we receive it?

It all came down to the restorative justice circle.

"All right," Sujatha said as she sat down on our couch after dinner. "If we're going to be ready for this circle Tuesday, we have a lot to talk about."

That night we discussed the details of the circle, but the conversation turned personal when Andy asked Sujatha how she had gotten into the restorative justice business in the first place.

She told us that when she was in college at Harvard, she planned to go to law school because she wanted to become a prosecutor and put child molesters behind bars. It was personal for her because her own father had sexually abused her when she was young.

Then one summer she traveled to India with her then boyfriend. He was starting a school in Mumbai. There she met women and children who had been abducted and forced to work as sex slaves. It was hard to listen to her talk about such dehumanizing conditions. She had a passion in her voice that I admired. She had even spent time with Mother Teresa, serving the poorest of the poor through her ministry.

"I even considered becoming a Catholic nun," Sujatha said with a laugh. I wondered if her boyfriend had known how the trip had affected her.

The trauma of spending time with the sex slaves and their children threatened to overcome her. Obviously, she was dealing with unresolved issues related to her own childhood abuse, which couldn't be undone simply by trying to help other people with theirs. Her fury and rage began to take a toll on her. She talked of suffering from blinding migraines, terrible stomach problems, and complicated relationships. And so, on the advice of some friends, she grabbed a backpack and hiked north to the Himalayas. She landed in the Dharamsala, where she was quite the anomaly, an Indian American traveling alone with a backpack. A number of Tibetan families in exile welcomed and befriended her. They wanted to know her story, and she wanted to know theirs.

Their stories gave her a new, life-shifting perspective. They told her about losing family members as they tried to escape the Chinese Army, about women getting raped, and children being made to kill their own parents, parents being forced to leave the bodies of their children behind, and worse.

Once again I was overwhelmed by the depth of pain some are made to endure in this world.

"I had to ask them," Sujatha continued. "How can you go through all of that and still have a smile on your face? You've been through so much. So why do you seem to be happier than I am? And time and time again, the response was the same: 'We practice forgiveness.'"

"I thought they were insane," she said. "I thought some things are just unforgivable!"

The woman who managed the guesthouse in which she was staying asked her, "Why are you so angry?"

Sujatha shared her story of abuse.

"She told me, 'People often write to His Holiness the Dalai Lama for advice. You should try it. Write the letter, then take it to his monastery. You'll get some sort of response.'"

Andy and I were rapt with attention. The Dalai Lama? That would be like writing a letter and putting it in the pope's mailbox.

"I wrote, 'Anger is killing me, but it motivates my work. How do you work on behalf of abused and oppressed people without anger as the motivating force?'

"I dropped the letter off at the front gate to the Dalai Lama's compound, but I didn't expect anything to come of it. I came back a week later, however, to see if there was a response. I figured I'd get some sort of prayer cord or a preprinted card. To my surprise, I was taken all the way in to his private secretary. 'His Holiness was moved by your letter, and his schedule has changed so he's not traveling this week,' the secretary said, while looking at a calendar. 'Would you like to have a private audience with him on Thursday?'"

Sujatha told us that she couldn't believe what she was hearing, but within days, she sat face-to-face with the Nobel Peace Prize winner. Sujatha began the conversation by talking about sexualized violence against women and children. She told him about her work counseling women and children who had been forced into sexual slavery.

"I told him about my father's abuse. How that was the motivation for me to do good in the world. But that the anger was having physical effects on me now. His Holiness listened attentively to my story, then he shared a very personal story about how he dealt with his own anger toward the Chinese. I was amazed by his ability to forgive and how peaceful he was.

"Then, when I asked His Holiness for specific advice on how to forgive my father, he asked me a genuine but profound question. 'Do you feel you have been angry long enough?' The question struck me. For a few moments I didn't respond. We sat in silence as I thought about the way anger had affected my life. My anger was killing me. The migraines and the stomach problems. I was a mess! So I finally simply said yes.'

"'Then, I have two pieces of advice for you.' He smiled at me. 'First, you should meditate. Second, open your heart to your enemies,' he said.

"'I'm just about to start law school to become a prosecutor so I can make sure that abusers, batterers, and child molesters all end up behind bars,' I protested. 'I'm not opening my heart to anyone!'"

The Dalai Lama thought her response was absolutely hilarious. "Okay," he chuckled and patted her on the knee. "Okay, okay, then you just meditate."

Inspired by the conversation, she went back to the United States and signed up for a ten-day meditation course conducted completely in silence.

"Then, on the very last day there," Sujatha told us, "I was able to completely forgive my father. I let go of all the hatred and just felt love for him."

Honestly, as I listened to this incredible story, I probably thought the same thing that others do when they hear our story. How could she have done this after just ten days of meditation? Could she really feel love for her father after what he'd done to her? But it was true. I could tell by the way she told the story, the sound of her voice. She felt it.

A couple of weeks after she had forgiven her father and returned home, she started law school. Without the rage of her abuse brewing in her soul, she no longer had the desire to become a prosecutor. Instead she decided to become an attorney who defends women who kill their abusers. "I didn't realize lawyers don't have the option of specializing in such a way," she said. "So once I became a defense attorney, I had to defend everyone—including people accused of child abuse. I found myself following His Holiness's second piece of advice, to open my heart to people I'd previously seen as my 'enemies.' And I learned that their life stories were not so different from my own."

Sujatha had benefited so immensely from forgiveness, but ultimately she was dissatisfied with how the system seemed bent on artificially segregating the victims and the perpetrators. Frequently, her clients simply wanted to apologize for the harm they had caused.

"I'd have to tell my client, 'Everything you say will be used against you. If you talk to the victims, it could be used against you if we get you a new trial,'" she said. "'Tell your therapist, and tell your priest, but you can't say a word to the victim.'"

Of course, this effectively squelched the potential for the restoration and emotional peace that frequently follows an apology. Sujatha couldn't quite reconcile this with what she'd learned in her spiritual practice. Victims frequently want to hear those words—I'm sorry—and criminals so desperately need to say them. Yet she denied them the opportunity because of legal posturing. Wasn't there a way to pursue justice outside of the adversarial roles of the criminal justice system? Somewhere in the middle?

This is how Sujatha was led to restorative justice, which led her right to my front door.

CHAPTER 16

*B*ring him in."

When Conor entered the room, we all stood. He looked at us awkwardly, as if he didn't know what to do. He was in the same room with people he loved. No glass to separate him from us. He looked down at his feet. His ankles weren't shackled.

We'd planned every detail with Sujatha—things such as who would sit where and who would walk in first.

"It's important for the victims to feel safe and comfortable in the room," she'd explained as we went over the minutiae of the meeting. "These decisions are commonly made before restorative justice circles so that everyone knows what to expect." Some of these details didn't strike us as particularly important. Neither Andy nor I felt that being in the room first would make us feel safer. Gradually, something occurred to me that Sujatha had not addressed.

"Will Conor be shackled?"

"Do you want him to be?"

Suddenly overwhelmed, I couldn't speak.

Sujatha waited patiently. She didn't know what I'd say, and neither did Andy. But I knew. My silence was due to pure emotion, not indecision. I couldn't even think of having them humiliate Conor in that way. Meeting face-to-face meant meeting person-to-person. I didn't need to prove anything by having Conor bound when he was brought into the room.

"No," I said through tears.

I could hear the surprise in Sujatha's voice. "Are you sure?"

"I'm not afraid of him," I said.

And so, he walked into the room freely, into a room with his mom and dad and us—the people who probably would have become his mother- and father-in-law. It was against the rules to touch inmates, but we had requested an exception be made for this circle.

"Go hug your mother," Sujatha said to Conor, who immediately walked over to his mom. He hadn't touched her in fifteen months. A lump formed in my throat. I watched as he hugged his dad, before he walked across the room to me. We embraced.

The last time I'd touched Conor, my daughter was alive. I wanted my hug to convey my forgiveness and my love for him. I was immensely sad for this young man whose previous life was over. Everything he could have been, he now had no chance to become. But I wanted him to know that we believed in redemption for him. We still visited Conor, so this wasn't the first time we had seen him in fifteen months. But it was the first time we were able to physically touch him.

The hugs were not overly emotional. No one cried. Since there were so many people there, it was a little awkward. This was not the time for a true reunion for anyone. That's the thing about prison . . . Conor had nothing but time, but not in the moments he truly wanted to last. It's like being thirsty when surrounded by a saltwater sea.

We were there for a purpose—not to have a tearful reunion or to bind up the gaping wounds he'd inflicted on us, but for the very tough business of determining Conor's fate. By the end of our meeting that day, we could all walk away with a sentence we'd agreed on that might give him a future outside the walls of the jail.

"Let me explain a little about what is going to happen here today," Sujatha said after everyone was seated. In the chair to the left of the doorway was Helene Potlock, Victim Assistance Program Director at the state attorney's office. Though she had dutifully taken notes in our prior meetings with Jack Campbell, and she had helped us apply for victim's aid for counseling, she never spoke much. Especially on this day. Beside her was a television and DVD player on an old metal rolling stand. Behind Andy and me was a long westward-facing window, so the sun poured into the room. I regretted wearing a blouse that wasn't cotton. It was the first day of summer for the rest of the nation, but we'd had summer for quite some time already. Jack Campbell and Greg Cummings sat along the south wall, Conor's parents faced us, Conor sat next to his mother, and Father Mike sat next to Conor. Sujatha completed the circle. The deputy sheriff sat outside the room at the desk the entire time. He was "off-duty," paid by the McBrides as part of the conditions of being able to conduct the circle at the jail.

The room was twelve by twelve and was made of concrete blocks. The only color in the room was the gray-speckled, white vinyl tiles on the floor. I was told we were sitting in stackable, plastic chairs instead of nicer wooden ones, in case things got intense. The plastic ones weren't as dangerous.

"We will begin the meeting with prayer, then State Attorney Jack Campbell will read the charges against Conor. Father Mike will speak about the impact on the community, then Andy and Kate will talk about Ann and what it meant to lose her. Conor will give a full account of what happened and answer any questions we have. After everyone has had a chance to speak, we will all discuss what we feel the terms of the sentencing should be and come to an agreement."

The room, warmed by the Florida sun, was silent.

The phrase "full account" was what got me. Since Ann's death, I couldn't really imagine how Conor—the boy we loved, invited into our home, and even employed—had killed the person he said he loved. He had given a confession the night he'd turned himself in, and the sheriff's detective had shared it with us. But I still couldn't imagine what had taken him from being a young man in a rocky teenage relationship to prison. In normal criminal proceedings, the details of the crime that might be held against the defendant are withheld. As I tried to brace myself for the inevitable emotional onslaught, I tried to remind myself that this was an honor—an opportunity to hear the truth.

"I've brought a picture of Ann," Sujatha said, holding up a photo. Taken during a happier time, it showed Ann sticking out her tongue at the person taking the photo. "If anyone starts behaving in a way that Ann would not like, then Andy and Kate are going to flash the picture."

Everyone nodded.

"We will be using a 'talking piece,'" she said. Sujatha had thought carefully about this object and had, with our permission, selected an item that reflected our story: Sophie the giraffe from the baby boutique. In a way, this teether had come to represent our last interaction with Ann. She had suggested I buy it for the baby shower; and Andy had gone by the store, bought the giraffe, and shared a chicken finger sub from Publix with Ann the day before she was killed. It seemed right to use a sweet, innocent object in such a way.

"Sophie will be passed from person to person around the circle. If you have Sophie, you have the floor and may speak without interruption. You may also hold the talking piece in silence or simply pass it on to the next person. It's up to you.

"Basically, using the talking piece will slow down our conversation, give everyone an equal voice, and give us time and space to express our emotions, even strong emotions," she said. "It will also allow for deeper conversation. No one should interrupt. Also, there is no outside discussion. If you have something to say, everyone needs to hear it. Let's begin."

Father Mike bowed his head. We all held hands.

"Father, we thank you for this opportunity to come here together today, to open our hearts to one another. Help us to make this a place of healing. God, please let us feel the presence of the Holy Spirit, send wisdom to guide us," Father Mike said. "Allow the peace and love of Jesus Christ to surround us . . ."

While Father Mike prayed, I whispered a prayer too.

"Come, Holy Spirit. Come, Holy Spirit. Come, Holy Spirit. Be here with us to guide everyone in the room," I said. "Amen."

Jack Campbell read the charges.

"Conor McBride has been charged by the state of Florida with first-degree murder and the discharge of a firearm in the commission of a felony."

Though the death penalty was not applicable for Conor's crime, we had heard that State Attorney Willie Meggs was pushing for a forty-year sentence.

Sujatha asked Father Mike to speak about the effect of Ann's death on the community. "When one member of the community is lost, the whole community grieves. We are all connected to one another. Death has touched us, and we are forever changed by that. And when it happens to someone so young, it is overwhelming. Someone so young, so vibrant. And not just one life has been taken by this act. Conor now faces a lengthy prison sentence. He will be sent away from his family, his friends. Certainly the parents, who have been devastated by the loss, suffer greatly. So many of us are left to question how such a thing can happen in our city. To our friends and our neighbors. How do we process this?"

As he spoke, I lamented that we didn't have a representative from the domestic violence activism community in the circle with us. We'd reached out to them but received no response. Using restorative justice in domestic violence cases is a touchy subject. Abusers are seen as masters of manipulation, and the fear is that they will do what they do best—apologize and then return to their negative behavior.

When it was time for Andy and me to talk, I unfolded a piece of paper that had all the information I wanted to cover. Our job was simple. We were to take this opportunity to truly explain to Conor what he'd done, what he'd taken from us. We did that by simply telling the story of Ann.

"I knew Ann would be a girl even though I only had one ultrasound very early in the pregnancy. We named her Ann Margaret the day after she was born, even though Sarah and Allyson preferred Rainbow Dolphin Star Heart.

"That would have been some name to grow up with," I said, using a line from our eulogy for Ann. People in the circle smiled.

"When she was a little baby, I carried her around in a baby sling all the time. So much so that when she eventually began walking, someone told me that they didn't think she had legs because they had never seen them. She was likely going to be our last baby, and everyone thought I would nurse her 'forever.' But she weaned when she was around eighteen months old.

"When she was eight years old, she was diagnosed with amblyopia," I said. "This is often called lazy eye. One eye sees better than the other, so the weaker eye shuts down. For two years we worked to recover her vision, patching her good eye so the weak one would work harder. We wanted her to be able to drive, to not be restricted from achievement because of her vision."

I remembered how much she hated wearing that patch, but I would gently remind her that it would help her see better in the future. I remember, too, that the stares and the questions made her more compassionate to her friends who may have also received stares because of braces or glasses.

Every restorative justice circle has a centerpiece or a focal point. Ours was the afghan that Ann's friend Khadijah had crocheted. When Ann was in the hospital, I'd put it at the foot of her bed. Now it rested at our feet, holding items we'd brought from home to represent her life.

There was the portrait the funeral home had created from her photo. We had also placed on the afghan a small box of mementos she'd collected in special moments: fall leaves, seashells, rocks. Plus, a plaster cast that my friend Cindy made of her uninjured hand while she was at the funeral home. This was an especially close reminder of her, because it had touched her and even had taken the shape of a part of her.

Andy picked up Ann's "Thespian of the Year" drama award and held it up as he shared.

"She found her niche in the Leon High School drama department. She didn't want to be the star of the stage; she loved the unseen work of stage management. We were the proud parents pointing to the stage during scene changes, saying: 'That's my daughter—there in black, pushing the scenery around.' Or, 'That buzzer you just heard? That was Ann.' We were proud of her backstage work and her awards for student direction. She had a feel for things like blocking—where the actors should stand on stage—and a desire to make sure things were done right. We loved hearing how much she contributed to the drama department and how reliable she was in getting things done."

Conor sat there silently as we talked. The weight of our words fell heavy on him.

"She was great at her job at the baby boutique too. Her boss told me she was confident leaving Ann in charge of the store. An eighteen-year-old who loved working in a baby boutique. We never quite understood her love of Sophie," I said, holding up the teether.

Andy and I were very teary and emotional as we talked about Ann's life, but we were also very proud of her. It was a joy to talk about her life and what she meant to us. When I started transitioning to her future—what might have been—my voice got shakier.

"We were certain that someday, Ann would have children of her own. Grandchildren that we'll never know now," I said, tears now falling. I noticed Julie wiping away her own tears. They would have been her grandchildren, too, had Conor and Ann gotten married.

Andy continued. "She was barely nineteen when she died. She was looking forward to going to the University of Central Florida. She was becoming a young woman. Really, she was still in that place where parents were mostly uncool."

My mind raced back to Andy's last communication with Ann. She was rushing through the house, and she asked Andy what he was making for dinner. Boring grilled chicken.

"Will you make me fettuccine Alfredo?" she had asked. Andy's specialty—made with half-and-half and Italian cheeses—was her favorite meal.

"No," he had responded. "We're having chicken for dinner. This isn't a restaurant."

She was upset. "Come on, Dad!"

"Do you see menus here?"

"But I'm going out on a picnic with Conor to celebrate making the dean's list, and I need to be able to take it with me."

When Andy saw how much it meant to her, his heart softened

toward his daughter and his resolve melted away. Though he wished she'd just eat what he was making her, he realized this was not a battle to fight.

"Okay, Ann," he told her. After all, what father can refuse his daughter?

He made her what she wanted and put in an extra portion for Conor. He had no idea this would be the last time he would interact with his daughter. This would be her last meal.

"In retrospect, I'm very thankful I made the fettuccine," Andy told the people in the circle.

I recalled the day the police released her car from evidence. The containers, with remnants of the meal, were still in the backseat.

"We were in the phase of parenting where everything was a battle," I explained. "We never had the chance to become her friends again."

"Becoming 'empty nesters' was something I was looking forward to," I said. "Instead, it was forced on me. From now on every holiday will have an empty seat at the table. Every family picture incomplete. There is a space that can never be filled."

I continued. "Ann sought Jesus in her own unconventional way. She had a quiet devotion to St. Anthony, the patron saint of horses. A Franciscan love of animals. A compassionate heart. She wanted her own wildlife refuge—St. Margaret's—where she would rescue horses and raptors. She'll never have the chance to do the good in this world that she was intended to do. Conor, you have to make up for that—you have to do the good works of two people now."

We also read a letter from my sister Patti, about how Ann had asked her to be her godmother. Since Ann had been baptized when we were attending a Methodist church, she did not have one. Patti also talked about the profound effect of being at the hospital and being in the room when Ann died. It was the catalyst that led to her sobriety after years of drinking.

After I finished the letter, we sat quietly and listened to "Angel Band" by the Stanley Brothers, which was as much Ann's song as the one that had been dedicated to her memory.

The song ended, and the room was filled with thick silence.

"What do you want to know?" Conor asked.

CHAPTER 17

"I want to know everything that happened and why it happened,"
Andy said. "From the moment she left the house with the fettuccine until . . ."

His voice trailed off. I knew Andy couldn't go further to actually say the words, "until she was shot." Not in this moment. Not
on this day.

All eyes in the room moved from the grieving father to the
offender.

At this point in the circle, Conor was supposed to explain what
had happened, to give us closure on the events that had transpired
that night. Usually in the criminal justice system, the offender and
the victims are forever separated, an effort to protect the victims
from being further damaged. The offender is coached to never
admit any wrongdoing, no matter what. However, this artificial
construct leaves no room for an apology from the offender. How
often do we read that the prisoner standing before the judge showed
no emotion at the trial or at sentencing? Victims are left to think
that the offenders have no remorse for their actions.

Because of this legal wall, it is often impossible for family
members to learn what really happened when their loved one died.

What were their last words? Andy wanted answers to those questions. By knowing, he felt he could somehow come to peace with what happened.

Restorative justice circles and Victim Offender Dialogue (VOD) programs provide the space for victims and their loved ones to have a voice . . . a place for offenders to take responsibility for their actions. This is why we'd come.

In all the times we had spoken to Conor at the Leon County jail, we had never spoken about this. Conor was under strict orders from his defense attorney not to speak to anyone about what had happened. He wasn't even sure what we knew. Had we read the police report? Seen his confession? What would we do, now that he was going to share with us the details of what he had done? He had no idea. But he did have a baby's faith. Faith in the God that the Grosmaires had shown him. The God who loves unconditionally.

Before he spoke, he leaned forward and placed his elbows on his knees. He looked directly at us, then cleared his throat as if to steady his voice.

"Ann and I would fight sometimes," he started, "because I didn't understand the things that were important to her. I would forget about meeting her for lunch and she would be so disappointed. We would argue, and we couldn't stop. Neither of us could let it go."

As he spoke, he described the typical things teens fight about. Honestly, the things over which I, as an adult, find myself being disappointed.

"Did they fight?" the detective had asked. *Don't all teens fight?* I thought. Ann was emotional, like me. I'd had my share of teenage arguments when I'd been caught up in the high emotions of the moment. I remember feeling like a breakup was the end of the world . . . crying behind a locked door while my mom stood on the other side, gently asking if everything was okay. I'd asked Ann the same question before.

"I hit her," Conor said, distressed by the memory of his explosive anger. "I hit her two times—two different occasions. Once in the stomach and once in the face. With my fist . . . each time." He explained that they'd both been horrified by his actions. Each time he was sorry for what he had done. Neither of them understood why he had reacted so violently. "We were scared to tell anyone. We were afraid of what might happen, that I might be arrested."

"Did you know he'd hit her?" the detective had asked. No, we hadn't. She hadn't even told her sisters. How many times had I thought about the fight Conor had with his dad? Conor had seemed so distraught. It didn't occur to me that Conor was learning by example. Fear and shame. Feeling isolated. Afraid to seek help.

He began to talk about what had happened that weekend. How Ann had planned a picnic dinner to celebrate her making the dean's list. She had expected congratulations, maybe a card, some sort of recognition—not just a dinner partner. Once again he had failed to understand how important it was to her.

He didn't care, she claimed.

He couldn't read her mind, he replied.

They had returned to his parents' house and began an argument that continued until he fell asleep from exhaustion.

He woke up to find her even angrier than she had been the night before. Neither of them had the maturity to walk away or to declare a cooling off period. Ann finally said she was leaving, then walked out of the house.

Conor sat there for a moment before saying more. "I was unsure if Ann meant she was leaving for the moment or leaving for good. I saw that she had left her water bottle, and I took it out to her car."

Why, Conor, why? I thought when the detective told us about Conor leaving the house. He just had to give her back her water bottle? It was as if some dreadful tether held them together in this place.

"'I wish you were dead!' she shouted at me. 'Okay,' I said. I went back into the house. I got my dad's shotgun and loaded it. I placed the barrel of the gun under my chin. *If I kill myself, would Ann blame herself?* I thought." A knock on the door interrupted his thoughts.

"It was Ann, begging me to let her in. I set the gun down on a table in the entryway, unlocked the door, and opened it."

Now the question fighting to escape through my mouth was for Ann.

Why? Why did you go back to the door, insist on coming back into the house? You were in the car! You could've just driven away.

When I first heard the story from the detective, there just seemed to be so many places where it all could have changed, so many moments when a clearer head would have made a better choice. Hearing it now all again from Conor only reemphasized the insanity. Two young kids tumbling toward the edge of the cliff, grabbing a branch only to let it go and continue tumbling, tumbling, tumbling . . .

"We went back to my bedroom. When she realized I intended to kill myself, she told me that she didn't want to live either. That's when I went back to get the gun."

None of this was new information, but hearing him explain it chilled me to the bone.

"I came back to the room and she was slumped on the floor, sitting on her knees. I wanted to scare her. I started waving the gun around. 'Is this what you want?' I asked her. She said, 'No, I don't . . .' But I stopped waving the gun around . . . I pointed it at her . . . I pulled the trigger."

"Let me get this right," Andy said, leaning forward a bit in his chair.

Andy rarely gets angry. When he's anxious or worried, he grows still. He's like a stone statue, immovable, strong. But there's a softer side to Andy—the side I normally see—which was revealed as layer after layer of emotion was being ripped from him as he listened to Conor speak.

"You shot her while she was asking you not to?" he asked. "While she was on her knees?"

As I watched Andy, I realized that his paternal instincts were still very present, even though Ann was gone. His baby had been in danger. He would have protected her with his life, and there was no doubt by the look in his eyes, by the way he seemed to become larger just sitting there in the chair. But he hadn't been there—didn't know to be there. And his father-protector spirit was crushed. For the first time he realized what people meant when they talked about heartache, because his heart began to physically hurt.

"Yes," Conor answered.

My mind raced as he spoke.

He had said it, in his own words. In one crazy instant, he had aimed the gun and pulled the trigger.

"We need to take a break," Jack said. It was as if we were all under a spell of grief and regret, and Jack's announcement punctured it. People stood up from the plastic chairs and stretched. Sujatha reminded everyone that in order to keep the integrity of the circle, we shouldn't have side conversations outside the room. If we felt the need to say something, it should be shared with everyone in the circle.

Andy and I immediately walked out into the reception area, followed closely by Jack Campbell, who apparently had no intention of abiding by Sujatha's no talking rule.

"You don't have to go through any more of this. I can end it right now," he said. "Just say the word."

End it right now? I thought. *We just heard about our daughter's last conscious moments on Earth. How much worse does he think it will get?*

"We want to continue," I said. I hadn't worked for almost a year for this circle to just walk away from it now. Always for me the whole thing was bigger than the Grosmaires and the McBrides, bigger than this tiny room. We had unlocked the door and stuck our foot in. There was no direction but forward. I had borne the unbearable. The worst *was* over.

Sujatha approached us to remind us it would be best to keep the conversation all together. Before she had a chance to open her mouth, Jack cut her off.

"I'm talking to the Grosmaires right now. Move away." After she took the cue, he turned back to us. "You don't have to go back in there."

Andy repeated what I said: "We want to continue."

Jack acquiesced.

Now that the rule had been tossed out the window, we went up to Sujatha to tell her what had transpired between Jack and us.

"I thought it would make sense," Andy said. "I thought that somehow, something he said would explain what happened. He was waving the gun and his finger slipped . . . but there is no reason, no explanation . . . it will never make sense."

Andy had come face-to-face with the futility of asking why.

I had not come to the circle to find answers, to know exactly what happened to Ann. I knew enough to know that it would never make sense. While his heart ached for Ann, my heart ached for Andy, who thought that somehow this impossible question could be answered.

We filed back into the room, resituated ourselves on the plastic chairs, and yielded the floor back to Conor.

"After I shot Ann, I thought about killing myself," he said. "But I couldn't do it. I got in my car and just drove around. I didn't know what I was going to do, where I was going to go, so in the end, I drove to the police department.

"I'm so sorry. I'm so, so sorry." He looked at Andy and me, his eyes filled with the remorse that victims seldom see in their offender's eyes.

There it was.

He'd told us a story of two young people who had been caught up in their emotions. They'd wanted to leave, but for whatever reason, weren't able to. They were teenagers with teenage emotions. Their angry words and tears should've been a squabble, a quarrel, a breakup fight. But since there was a weapon present, this normal fight suddenly escalated into something people frequently called "an unimaginable tragedy."

Michael's eyes were rimmed in red, as Julie unfolded some papers she'd brought from home that contained her thoughts.

"I cannot believe that my son has caused such a great harm," she read, her voice full of raw emotion. In fact, she only got through about half a page before she abruptly stopped, looked up at us, and sighed. "That's all I want to say for now," she said, as if she were barely able to utter another word.

That meant that the floor was Michael's. He shifted in his chair; his turn had arrived a bit earlier than anticipated.

"I just want to say that I'm so sorry. If I ever thought that my gun would have harmed anyone, I would never have kept it in the house. I know that I've had anger issues for a long time. When my brother died almost ten years ago, I got angry with God and the world. I stayed angry, and now I've taught Conor how to be angry," he said regretfully. "I feel that I also have some responsibility in this. I wish I could've been charged with a crime and made to serve jail time with Conor, because of my anger."

"Wait," Jack Campbell interrupted—a forbidden gesture in the circle. Because everyone had been so respectful and polite while others talked, we hadn't had to use Sophie the giraffe as the talking piece. All of us turned, surprised to hear what he had to say.

"Sir, you are not responsible for what happened," he said. "Conor alone is the one who pulled that trigger."

We all knew what Jack meant. By the letter of the law, Michael was not guilty of any crime against the state. But the circle is also about harm caused to the community. He was willing to admit the effect that his anger had on his son. He wanted a place to express his sorrow for allowing his anger to control him for so many years. This was everyone's chance to say what they wanted to say, and I appreciated Michael's honesty.

I took a deep breath. I was still trying to process the details of Ann's last moments, but I knew what was coming next: the discussion of an appropriate sentence for Conor.

Before coming to this meeting, I'd told Sujatha I would offer five years, with conditions: anger management classes, community service, and speaking to the public about teen-dating violence.

After hearing what I'd just heard, five years seemed like an awfully short period of time.

Five years?

Had I really promised I would say that?

But I had no more time to consider, because Sujatha started with me. "Kate, what do you suggest as an appropriate sentence?"

I paused for a moment, as I knew this could determine Conor's fate. Was five years appropriate for ending someone's life? Ann's?

"Five . . . to *ten* years," I said. I felt as though I had to honor what I had previously stipulated, but I also had to honor Ann's life. Her last words.

No, I don't.

I felt the freedom to say five years, because we knew Conor would never be sentenced to such little time. I also knew this wasn't some sort of elementary math problem. Jack wasn't going to take everyone's recommendations and average them out. We didn't need a low number to help the curve. Like all negotiations, however, we needed to know what the bottom line was; and I suddenly wanted the bottom line moved up a little bit.

Sujatha looked at Andy. "And you?"

"Ten to fifteen years, followed by probation with conditions." Secretly, I was thankful he'd requested a higher sentence. I squeezed his hand.

Sujatha looked at the McBrides.

"We agree with the Grosmaires," said Michael.

That didn't make sense to me. I had said something entirely different than Andy. Did they agree with me or with him?

Father Mike just shook his head when Sujatha looked to him. Though he was the de facto community representative, he didn't feel that he had any authority to recommend a sentence.

"My fate is in your hands," Conor said, his head down.

He was right.

All eyes went to Jack Campbell, the man who was the deciding factor. He has light green eyes under thick eyebrows and the manner of someone who's seen it all.

What would he say? Offer the forty-year sentence the state attorney supposedly wanted? Would he come down five years for every five years we went up? Had his experience in the circle changed his outlook on what could be accomplished?

Instead of answering, however, he closed his notebook and stood up.

"Thank you all very much," he said. "I've heard your recommendations. I'll take them back to my office and review them with my boss. I'll let you know what's decided."

What?

We were supposed to have a discussion. If nothing else, this was a pre-plea conference. Shouldn't we walk away with the recommendation for the judge, just as if it were only Jack and Greg Cummings?

"Jack, it would be best if we could at least hear your initial thoughts at this time," Sujatha said. But Jack politely declined.

"Decisions like this should not be made when emotions are running so high," he said simply before exiting the room.

The circle had ended, and we were all left stunned.

We hugged Conor one last time. Everyone was too surprised by the abrupt ending to speak.

After we watched a deputy take Conor away, we gathered up Ann's things and put them back into the cardboard box. I carefully wrapped up the things she had found so precious, and we were escorted out.

It was a very quiet trip to the parking lot. Helene Potlock had disappeared with Jack, leaving everyone else to follow the deputy through the maze of hallways and out of the building.

"Thank you, Father Mike," Andy said, hugging him.

"It was quite something. I'm glad I could be here for you. God bless you both." He walked off to his car, too exhausted to say any more.

Greg Cummings had spoken briefly to the McBrides and left just as quickly.

"We're going to need some time to process everything," Sujatha said. She knew we were all disappointed by the sudden ending of the circle. "We'll talk in the morning," she said to the McBrides, then she and Andy and I went out to dinner.

"How could he just leave like that? That was not in the spirit of the circle. That was not what was supposed to happen! We were supposed to reach an agreement. Everyone was going to agree on the sentence and it would be taken to the judge. What just happened, Sujatha?"

She sat silently in the restaurant and allowed us to express our frustrations.

"There should have been a beginning, a middle, and an end,"

I said. "There was a beginning and a middle, and now I feel as if I am just dangling there."

My disappointment was crushing. Had the circle been a success? All the praying, the petitions, the planning. And now we were playing another waiting game. Not knowing if anything we said or did in that room would matter. That disappointment remained with me all evening and into the following days.

When we got back to our home, I poured some tea. We sat in our living room and evaluated what had happened.

"At least now I have no more questions," Andy said. "I don't have to wonder if there was anything I could have done, or any way I could have prevented what happened."

We sat in silence.

"How do you feel about forgiving Conor now?" Sujatha asked me, quietly. "You know, now that you have heard everything."

I took a sip of tea and sighed.

"Honestly," I said, "I'll have to think about it."

CHAPTER 18

Forgiveness isn't an event; it's a lifestyle.

I've found that—after the big decision to forgive was made—it continued to happen, step-by-step, as new information came up or new thoughts came to mind. We had to forgive Conor when he told us he'd shot Ann while she was on her knees. We had to forgive Ann for going back inside the house. Why didn't she just drive away? She was free and clear. She'd be alive now. We had to forgive Conor for hitting Ann. We had to forgive Ann for not coming to us when Conor hit her. We had to forgive the McBrides for not realizing what was going on with Conor. We had to forgive Michael for having a gun in the house—though locked—which Conor could access.

When these things came up, we had to remind ourselves: *we have already forgiven this.*

Frequently Conor would say to me, "Thank you for forgiving me." My response was always the same. "I didn't do it for you. I did it for me."

Of course, I know forgiveness benefits both of us. But what I was trying to convey to Conor was this: forgiveness is an emotional release for the forgiver.

After all, I have a husband and two other living children. I had to forgive Conor because I had a life to live. One day I hope to have grandchildren. Because of the people in my life, I couldn't allow myself to be stuck in a place of bitterness.

∽

Everyone has their year in court.

A couple of weeks after our restorative justice circle, we still hadn't heard from Jack Campbell. Ann had been gone for more than a year, which—of course—was a long period of time to be without closure. After the pre-plea conference, we talked to Sujatha, biding our time by analyzing every possible outcome, every eventuality.

"I never necessarily wanted Conor to receive a lighter sentence, but I did want his sentence to be meaningful," I had told her before the pre-plea conference. "If the state wanted him to spend twenty-five years in prison, for example, then perhaps half of those years could be spent behind bars while the other half could be spent serving the community."

"I know," Sujatha said. Of course, we'd gone through all this before we even stepped foot in the restorative justice circle.

"I wish he could mow my yard for the rest of his life," Andy said. I could tell he was only half-joking. Conor was a guy who had gotten accepted into Stanford. Letting him rot away in jail wouldn't help him, Tallahassee, or us.

I wanted him to serve nonprofits for which Ann would have volunteered. As a matter of fact, we procured letters from four or five community organizations that stated they would allow Conor to perform community service with them. Plus, he could start restorative justice programs in prison and go to high schools—in shackles—to talk about teen-dating violence. We knew of a young man convicted of DUI manslaughter who had done just this—with the mother of one of the young women killed in the accident.

During this time of waiting, I wondered if all our efforts toward restorative justice had been futile. The plea agreements seem to work more like a car sale: *Let me take this to my manager and see what he says.* Jack Campbell said he would not make a decision until he received the approval from State Attorney Willie Meggs.

Meggs apparently was a hard-hitting prosecutor who Jack thought wouldn't sign off on any sentence less than forty years. Once Jack described how the circle worked—and assured him of our perspective—Meggs softened. Everyone knew this would be a controversial sentencing, so he just wanted to make sure that people were thinking logically about it. Additionally, Jack received input from community leaders and local domestic-violence shelters before making his decision. He felt the pressure of the present (as we all waited) and of the future (from people who might ask him how he'd come to this decision).

Finally, the plea offer came. Not one, but two offers. First, twenty-five years, day for day. Meaning Conor would receive no time off. No early release. Second, twenty years, day for day, followed by ten years of probation.

"What do you think?" Sujatha asked when she called after hearing of the offers.

I sighed. Michael had said that Conor was seriously considering the twenty-five-year offer. Serving five extra years would mean that once he was out, there would be no one looking over his shoulder. With a ten-year probation, he would run the risk of being sent back to prison for any infraction—even as minor as showing up late for an appointment.

"What about our terms of probation: anger management classes, volunteering, speaking on teen-dating violence? If he serves twenty-five years, then he's really not obligated to do those things," I said. Could I trust Conor to honor those conditions if they weren't required? I couldn't help but doubt. I wanted him to be out sooner. Only when he was released could he truly make amends for the harm he had caused. I realized that the threat of re-imprisonment was a real one. Could I blame him if he chose to walk out of prison after an additional five years with no obligation to the state?

We didn't have to wait long. After just a few days, Conor chose the sentence of twenty years with ten years of probation, plus the specific conditions we had requested. I was pleased. It wasn't exactly what we had wanted. Ideally, we had hoped that after negotiating, we would have settled on fifteen years followed by probation. But considering what would have happened had we done nothing, we couldn't help but feel satisfied with our accomplishment. We had unlocked the door to restorative justice and cracked it open. It could never be shut again.

Over the past year and a half, we had visited Conor regularly. Suddenly, a passage from Matthew 25 came alive to me in its practical life application. Tucked away in a series of parables is a sobering vision of the future of Jesus on the heavenly throne, with all the nations gathered before the divine authority and great judge. He separates the righteous from the unrighteous. How does Jesus tell who fits into the "righteous" category? Helpfully, he provides a list: "I was hungry and you gave me something to eat, I was thirsty and you gave me something to drink, I was a stranger and you invited me in, I needed clothes and you clothed me, I was sick and you looked after me, I was in prison and you came to visit me." Now, these folks hadn't actually ministered to Jesus in these ways; so when they ask him about this, Jesus explains, "Whatever you did for one of the least of these brothers and sisters of mine, you did for me" (vv. 35–40).

The "sobering" part comes when he talks to the "unrighteous":

"Then [the King] will say to those on his left, 'Depart from me, you who are cursed, into the eternal fire prepared for the devil and his angels. For I was hungry and you gave me nothing to eat, I was thirsty and you gave me nothing to drink, I was a stranger and you did not invite me in, I needed clothes and you did not clothe me, I was sick and in prison and you did not look after me.'

"They also will answer, 'Lord, when did we see you hungry or thirsty or a stranger or needing clothes or sick or in prison, and did not help you?'

"He will reply, 'Truly I tell you, whatever you did not do for one of the least of these, you did not do for me.'" (vv. 41–45)

It was relatively easy to go through life without even thinking about people in prison. I never encountered people who might go to jail or who have been in jail, so it was pretty easy to think of inmates as dangerous and scary. More accurately, it was easier to just simply not think of them at all. However, right there in the scriptures, Jesus enumerates what he's looking for in our lives. He wants us to:

1. Give food to the hungry.
2. Provide drink to the thirsty.
3. Welcome the lonely.
4. Clothe those in need.
5. Visit the sick and those in prison.

Note that visiting people in prison is 20 percent of what Christ mentioned! Obviously, the Christian life is not a matter of checking items off a list. But the book of James says that "works" always accompany a living, vibrant faith, meaning the Christian life will necessarily be poured out in service of the poor and downtrodden (James 2:14–20). When Conor went to jail, I realized—with a sudden immediacy—that I had not even considered the plight of the prisoner until I knew someone who had been incarcerated. And so, for the past year and a half, Andy and I regularly met with Conor in jail, using every one of the thirty minutes per visit we were allocated.

While we waited for the sentencing hearing, we discovered a state law that would throw a wrench in our plans. We were told that the state of Florida does not permit victims to visit offenders in the prison system. State prisons were under the jurisdiction of the Florida Department of Corrections, while the Leon County jail was run by the Sheriff's Office. While it was possible to apply for visitation, it would be a process—yet another hurdle we'd have to jump over. But here's the thing: I wasn't sure how long I wanted to keep visiting Conor. Learning of the rule was sort of a relief. We'd see Conor at the hearing, he'd go to prison, and that could be it. The decision would be made for us, and it would be out of our hands.

"Father Mike," I confessed, "at some point, haven't I done enough?"

"Kate, you have done more than enough." His voice took on a serious tone. "Don't ever think that you haven't done enough. You've done more than enough."

He just repeated this over and over, in the hopes of it sinking in.

Finally, after three weeks, it came time for sentencing. Instead of being a dramatic, emotional experience, it was very procedural.

Jack Campbell stood and highlighted the aggravating factors in the crime. Citing Conor's "domestic violence," he gave him a choice. He could either have a twenty-year sentence (with no time off for good behavior), plus ten years of probation; or he could choose twenty-five years in prison without probation. Conor took twenty years with probation. It was more time than we wanted, but far less than Jack would have offered if we hadn't pursued restorative justice. In a newspaper article, Jack was quoted as saying, "There's no way I would have—based on these facts and circumstances—agreed to a sentence this lenient had they not asked me and sincerely expressed to me how important it was to them to allow them to heal."[1]

Circuit Judge Charles Dodson then read Conor's sentence in front of the court, and added that he would also need to take an anger management class and talk to school groups about domestic teen violence or make a video to distribute to those types of groups.

We had a chance to speak. That day I'd worn my necklace with a Franciscan cross. Andy wore a blue shirt with a tie that prominently had the word *Hope* written on it. We walked up to the lectern and read from prepared statements.

"What then should be a payment for taking a life? That life in return? What purpose does it serve but to just create an empty space where two young lives are lost? Conor owes us a debt he can never pay. To expect him to be able to repay that debt will leave us wanting for the rest of our lives. Ann wanted peace for us," I said. "And that peace will come through forgiveness."

Conor had the chance to speak as well. "I apologize to everyone that I've hurt and everyone who has suffered because of my actions," he said. "As the Grosmaires said, I owe a debt I can't pay. But I'll give the rest of my life to make sure some good will come out of this."

Greg Cummings then said, "Judge, we would like for you to include your recommendation that the Grosmaires be allowed to visit Mr. McBride when he goes to prison."

Andy and I exchanged glances. We had no idea that he was going to make this request. Though we'd discussed whether or not we would want to jump through hurdles to see Conor once he went to a state correctional facility, there was a certain peace in allowing the law to form a barrier between us and the man who killed our daughter. Greg probably assumed we would want to keep up the visitation after all we'd done to go the route of restorative justice. But we weren't so sure.

The judge looked at us. "Mr. and Mrs. Grosmaire, do you want to visit Conor in prison?"

In that moment, a million things went through my mind. I thought, *Well, I can't say no because that will be binding forever. I probably need to say yes in order to hold open that opportunity.* I'm not sure what went through Andy's mind. But we had one second to make this rather large decision. Simultaneously, without consultation, we both said yes. For whatever reason, God has decided that we are to be a part of this young man's life. Though we weren't sure we would go out of our way to pursue this, there was also no way that we would—when asked—shut that door.

Consequently, the judge made a recommendation, but it would be up to the Department of Corrections for final approval. When the sentencing hearing was over, there were a few hugs, big sighs of relief, and media asking for interviews.

This part of our lives could now be put behind us.

Conor was led out of the courtroom and put back behind bars.

CHAPTER 19

*A*ndy was driving to church to meet my mom and me for a Wednesday night dinner. Because he was running late, he took a shortcut hoping traffic would be better by the city park. Suddenly, a large bird came from his left and flew right into the front fender of the Jeep. After the initial loud thud, he looked in the side mirror and saw a bird tossed up into the air before it landed on the road. It looked like a pile of feathers in the median.

Was that a Canada goose? he wondered.

Either way, that bird was a goner. Andy kept driving because he was running late. He made the next turn and headed up the main road to the church, but a sense of guilt came rushing over him. Ann, who loved birds so much, would have hated that he'd left a bird in the road. Since she would have definitely insisted he turn around and help it, he did a U-turn. It was against his better judgment. What bird could have survived that collision? Well, at least he wouldn't leave it in the middle of the street.

When he walked up to the dead bird, he noticed its brown feathers above, lighter feathers below, and its talon feet. He'd know it anywhere, since Ann could identify all the birds of prey in the

Florida area. Ann loved raptors, especially hawks . . . which was exactly what he'd just killed. A beautiful red-tailed hawk.

As he was looking at the bird, its body twitched. It was alive! Alive, but injured.

Surprised, Andy nervously took off his light jacket and wrapped it around the bird. The bird didn't move. So far so good. He picked up the bird and watched for a break in the heavy traffic.

People must think I'm crazy standing out here, he thought. He scuttled across the street and stepped up on the sidewalk. Right then, the hawk put its head out of the jacket and turned toward the car. At least the bird knew which direction they were going. Andy, looking at its sharp large beak, felt a sense of panic. When he finally made it to the Jeep, Andy had to put the bird down because the liftgate would not stay up.

Why didn't I get this liftgate fixed? he thought. *This is wrong in so many ways. What a father won't do for his daughter.* Lodging the liftgate with his shoulder, he bent down to pick up the bird and put it in the back of the Jeep.

Would it panic when put in the vehicle? Would it realize Andy was trying to help? Thankfully, St. Francis Wildlife Association had a drop-off location for injured or orphaned wildlife just a little more than a mile away.

Since he didn't have a box in which to keep the bird contained, he said a prayer.

"Ann, please keep this bird calm as I drive it to the animal hospital."

He pulled slowly out of the park and onto the road. As he drove, Andy was afraid to look into his rearview mirror. He imagined if he did, the hawk would be there saying, *Gotcha!*

At the animal hospital, Andy rushed into the emergency entrance and saw a young woman at the desk.

"I have an injured hawk in the car," he said. "Please help me."

The woman looked up from the desk and said, very calmly, "You'll have to bring it in, sir."

He thought, *Seriously? I have to bring in this huge raptor. Are you not trained to handle these birds?* "You know, it's a pretty big hawk," he said, more diplomatically than his thoughts. "I'm uncomfortable carrying the bird because it's loose in the back of my Jeep."

"Let me get you a box to help," she said. Andy was relieved, thankful to have assistance. When she came back into the room, she carried a box that a few baby chicks could've fit in.

"Not even close," he told her.

"Okay . . ." She looked at him skeptically. "Let's go see this bird of yours."

As they walked out together, Andy warned her. "It's only wrapped up in a jacket. It's basically loose in there."

She was unfazed, until Andy opened the gate.

"That's a big bird!" she gasped. "Wait here!"

She came back a few minutes later with a big box, picked up the jacket and bird in one motion, put them in the box, and closed the flaps. Inside one of the examining rooms, she was able to inspect the bird more carefully.

"We'll keep her here until the local wildlife rehabilitator comes by tomorrow to pick her up," she said. "Do you want your jacket back?"

He did, but he took one look at the claws entangled with the jacket, and thought better of it. However, he watch in amazement as the woman—with just a few quick movements—got the jacket and handed it back to him.

The hawk spent two weeks in rehabilitation at the wildlife center. A month later, we got a call from the rehabilitator who said the young female hawk was doing well. No bones had been broken.

"Would you like to be there when she's released?" he asked.

We wouldn't miss this. This young female hawk had begun to remind Andy of Ann—it was beautiful, sleek, and exhibited a spirit to live and soar again. Andy imagined Ann raising up from her hospital bed and soaring into freedom into the sky just like the hawks she loved so much.

On a sunny, cool Florida morning, we met at a popular baseball location, Winthrop Park—exactly where the hawk had flown into Andy's Jeep. The rehabilitator asked if Andy would like to hold the bird until it flew off. He said yes, but not so confidently after seeing her sharp beak and claws again. The rehabilitator put the hawk in Andy's gloved hands, and Andy broke into a full-blown grin. What an honor to be so close to such a magnificent bird! What an even greater honor that Andy was able to participate in saving its life. When he opened his hands, the hawk swooped almost to the ground, then flew up to the branch of a tree about fifty yards away. Andy watched the hawk for a few minutes and said silently to himself, *Thank you, Ann, for being here with me.* The rehabber said that she would most likely stay and make her home in the park. Spectators at the baseball field in the park have seen her flying overhead.

❧

After Ann died, my mom (not the most outgoing person) wanted to talk to Conor's mom. One afternoon I invited Julie over to the house. She and my mom went out on the back porch for close to three hours. They shared a terrible bond. Because my brother had accidentally shot his friend when he was a child, both she and Julie had sons who had killed someone else with a gun. I remember standing at the window, looking out into the yard, and marveling as I watched them talk.

An outside observer wouldn't have been able to notice anything amazing about two women sitting on the porch, chatting. But what was really happening was more profound, more delicate, and more powerful than almost anything I have ever seen.

One of the basic premises of restorative justice is that all our lives are connected in more ways than we imagine. That's why it's a travesty that we effectively throw away so many people into the gigantic cultural trash cans of prison.

Though the United States represents less than 5 percent of the world's population, we have more people in prison than any other nation in the world—almost 25 percent of all incarcerated people.[1] Over the past four decades, our rate of incarceration has increased by 540 percent, even though crime rates have fluctuated.[2] This sort of mass incarceration represents a serious crisis in the criminal justice system, especially since many inmates don't need to be in prison to ensure public safety. While some people—including Conor—are there for good reason, others are left languishing in a system because of mandatory sentencing requirements or to make politicians look as though they're "tough on crime."

When we put people in jail, we're effectively throwing people away. We're saying, "You are too complicated for society. We no longer want to see you or deal with you." But the truth is that these people (and let's face it, we are mostly talking about men) have connections to the community. Many leave behind spouses and significant others. They leave behind children, who no longer have fathers to provide for them. There are more victims of crime than the ones whose wallets are stolen. It affects us all.

But followers of Christ believe all people bear the *imago dei*, Latin for the "image of God." C. S. Lewis wrote, "There are no *ordinary* people. You have never talked to a mere mortal."[3] In other words, the people we encounter every day—the ones who cut us off in traffic, the ones with fifty items in the "25 items or less" lane, the ones we barely notice, and the ones we'd rather not see—have souls that will live forever. As the little children sing, "They are precious in his sight."

When we fail to see how interdependent all members of our

society are, we fail our culture. People are not disposable and they each have a role to play in the larger society.

When we fail to receive God's forgiveness, we fail ourselves. We don't have to be defined by the worst thing we've ever done in our lives.

When we fail to forgive others as God has commanded, we fail each other. We don't have to be victims our whole lives.

When my mom was talking with Julie in the backyard, I witnessed a "God moment"—a beautiful picture of how we are all connected, how we all affect one another, in big ways and small.

As they chatted, I remembered that moment years ago in Memphis when my mom was at lunch with some women who asked her where she lived. When she'd told them the road, a woman asked, "Oh, isn't that where the little boy was shot?" My mother, overcome with shame and guilt over the incident, had claimed she knew nothing about it.

Yet there she was, ministering openly to Conor's mom, sharing details of the experience that I probably had never heard. I'm sure it was as helpful for my mom to talk to Julie as it was for Julie to talk to my mom. In many ways it was a miracle that they—the grandmother of a murder victim and the mother of the killer— could even be civil to each other. Yet there they were. Connecting. Laughing. Crying. Overcoming.

There's just something about humanity. We were made to need each other.

At Ann's visitation people from our neighborhood, church, and community were lined up out the door. I remember we stood for almost three hours. People asked, "How could you just stand there for so long?"

"You know what?" I replied. "With so much support, I felt as if I was floating in love."

CHAPTER 20

*I*n 2012 Sujatha called to tell us that she had been contacted by
Paul Tullis, a writer for the *New York Times Magazine*, about
a story on restorative justice. Though we believed it would be
wonderful to share our story with such a large readership, Sujatha
met Paul and was a little hesitant about moving forward. She
was always so protective of us. Paul was clearly a liberal writer,
and Sujatha was concerned about how he might treat us. Always
cautious about the media, we had only shared our story with the
Catholic Compass, our diocesan magazine. We wanted to be sensitive to Conor and Ann's story, and we wanted to be sure a reporter
would handle it sensitively and without sensationalizing it. As far
as we knew, however, Conor's case was the first capital murder in
America to be resolved through restorative justice pre-adjudication
(before trial). Since we had to forge our own path through this
complicated wilderness, we felt an obligation to share our story in
a way that was accessible to others.

"Paul Tullis," I typed into my computer the day before he was
supposed to arrive. I wanted to familiarize myself with this reporter's
work so that I wouldn't be caught off guard with his questions.
When I found his Twitter account, I read through some of his

past tweets, which weren't at all surprising: he definitely had the air of a "rock-star reporter." We were aware that we lived in the well-established stereotype of "flyover country." Would a writer from Los Angeles be able to understand our faith and how it animates our lives? Would he treat us like individuals, or some sort of Southern stereotype? Of course, I am from Pennsylvania and grew up in Memphis before moving to Tallahassee; Andy's parents are from New York and Nebraska. Though neither of us has any sort of entrenched Southern nature, I believe it's hard for people to separate us from our geography.

Then, to my surprise, I read some tweets that seemed to apply to our case. Such as, Here's a first: I'm composing a letter to a convicted murderer (for my article on #restorativejustice for a major US weekly magazine).[1] Then, the day before he met us, he tweeted asking for advice:

> In 3 hrs, I'll be meeting a killer's parents and his victim's parents at the same time. Any advice? #journalism #reporters #newspapers

Over the course of five days, he met with all the key participants in the circle and interviewed several of Ann's friends. On his last day he had a final interview with Andy and me at our house. When he arrived, we showed him Ann's room and pointed out a little table we set up that includes some of the things we took to the restorative justice circle. We thought the interview was going pretty well, until we got to the part where we were discussing the restorative justice process. Andy explained that our process meant that Conor didn't have to go to trial.

"Which is good," Paul said. "Because they invariably would've used the *bitch-deserved-it* defense."

Paul was referring to a legal strategy that blames the victims for their own abuse: the abuser's behavior is at least understandable, considering how intolerable the victim was. Jack Campbell had also expressed that the defense would paint Ann in a negative light, but he certainly never said it like this.

Paul wasn't saying Ann did deserve to die. In fact, he was saying that avoiding trial probably saved us from a great deal of grief. This much was true. But when he said the word *bitch*, Andy stiffened in his chair. Almost as soon as he said the words, Paul excused himself for a bathroom break. Andy leaned over to me and said sternly, "He needs to leave." Though I scarcely could imagine a less sensitive way to talk about this topic to the parents of a murdered child, what would happen if we kicked a *New York Times* reporter out of our home? Would that be the end of the article? I wanted our message of forgiveness and restorative justice to be told. Was it worth it to pass up that opportunity?

I whispered a protest, but Andy was adamant. Paul had crossed a line.

He came back into the room and was about to begin interviewing us again, when Andy said, "Can you wait a second before turning back on your recording device?"

"Sure," Paul said, looking up at us in surprise.

"I'm going to have to ask you to leave," Andy said. "No one will come into my house and use the word *bitch* when referring to my daughter."

Paul's face fell.

"Listen," he said. "I am so sorry for my poor choice of words. I really—really—didn't mean to offend you. As soon as I said the words, I knew it was wrong. I think that's why I had to get out of the room."

Andy looked at Paul's stricken face. There were tears in his eyes.

Andy studied the reporter for a good long time, assessing him. "All right, I forgive you. You can start recording again."

I had been watching Paul, but I turned to Andy. He had gone from hurt and offended father and back to interviewee just like that. All it took was for Paul to be sorry for what he'd done and to offer a sincere apology.

When the interview was over, Andy walked Paul to his car. There Andy gave him one of his bear hugs before Paul drove off. We ended up building a really good relationship with Paul, and we appreciated how he had responded with sincere remorse.

He did a great job with the article. Originally, it was scheduled to be the cover article of the *New York Times Magazine*, but the political situation at the moment was too complicated. The recent tragic shooting at Sandy Hook Elementary School in Connecticut had embroiled the nation in a terrible argument over guns, safety, and politics. The editors didn't want to publish a cover story about a murderer under the headline "Forgiven," considering the country's raw feelings. Though it wasn't a cover story, it caused a lot of national conversation and was the second-most e-mailed story from that edition.

⟡

In her Seattle home a woman opened the *New York Times Magazine* article and read it with intense interest. She scoured the story, wondering if the lessons we'd learned and the road we'd paved could possibly help in her legal case.

In May of the previous year, she and her husband were going out of town together for the first time since she'd given birth to their two children, who were five and seven years old. They'd arranged for her husband's parents to come in from California to babysit the children, but they needed to run a few errands first. Her husband, a high-level software engineer, loaded the kids into their van and went to pick up a few things, accompanied by his mom and dad.

When he stopped at a red light around 4:30 p.m., his father noticed gunfire erupting on the street. Then, after he heard the shots, he realized the van was rolling through the intersection. He looked over at his son, who was in the driver's seat, and saw that he'd been shot in the head. A gang member's bullet had made its way through the air, into their van, and into his son. His dad unbuckled his seat belt, stopped the car, and held his son. His mother ran to get help, leaving the children strapped into the car with their dying father. Their grandfather cradled their father as he died.

When the woman read our story, she was inspired by how we'd sat down with Conor and forgiven him face-to-face. She asked the defense attorney about meeting with the twenty-one-year-old whose stray bullet had killed her husband. Of course, they had never done anything like that before, and they were nervous about putting the widow and the shooter in the same room. After trying unsuccessfully to use a restorative justice facilitator from Oakland, they had to create their process from scratch. One year after the shooting, however, in a courtroom full of lawyers, police officers, and jail guards, she had the chance to talk to the shooter directly. He was a high school dropout, with gang tattoos on his arm and neck.

She explained how her husband being killed right in front of his parents and children affected her family. Since he'd already pled guilty, he really had nothing to gain by participating in this process.

However, he was a dad too. He felt he owed it to the woman—and even to his own daughter—to face what he had done. After reading her statement, she let him speak. He apologized and seemed to be deeply affected by the interaction. His attorney said he cried for days after the meeting. The King County Superior Court judge was not as affected by his remorse. A few days later, he sentenced the man to twenty-three years in prison, which was four years longer than the prosecutors had requested and was the maximum available under state law.

This story shows how restorative justice is not a cookie-cutter response to crime, but rather a process that plays out in different ways within different situations. Certainly this woman's letter to the offender affected the way he felt about what had happened. Being accountable for what you have done because you understand the personal consequences is a critical part of restorative justice. Additionally, this case shows that restorative justice isn't always about getting a lighter sentence. Rather, it's a more personal approach to justice. Lastly, I'm not sure if this woman decided to forgive the person who took her husband's life, but restorative justice doesn't require, encourage, or coerce victims to forgive the offenders.

I think Sujatha put it best: "Restorative justice never requires forgiveness as a prerequisite for participation or as an outcome. We don't want to put pressure on victims to forgive. But I can't think of a better cauldron for cooking up some forgiveness than a restorative process."[2]

In fact, as I think about the main legacy of Ann's life, I know it will be about challenging people to forgive. During the five years since her death, Andy and I have spoken to organizations and churches to share our message all over the country.

It's had an effect on people. We hear inspirational stories of people who have been victimized by intimate partner abuse and have lived robust lives afterward. In fact, a few days after the shooting, we received a letter from a hospital worker who had been present the day Ann was shot.

She wanted us to know that she had been praying for us, and that she had been affected by our calmness during such a horrible tragedy. Ann had been one of her first trauma patients, but she had felt the Lord's presence with us in the Emergency Room. She then went on to describe a past relationship that involved such extreme intimate partner abuse that she herself had been the one who landed in the Emergency Room. Now she has a wonderful husband and has forgiven her ex-boyfriend. She was thankful to have found comfort in our strength.

Also, I had a friend who had a distant relationship with her mother. Though they lived in the same town, she never liked seeing her or spending time with her because of many challenging incidents from her childhood. Several months after Ann's death, she told me that she could not call herself my friend and ignore my message of forgiveness. She forgave her mother for all the hurts of her childhood. In her case, the forgiveness happened in her heart. Her mom probably would have been confused by a confrontation, so my friend just decided to let go of the hurt and forgive her mom. Afterward she felt so liberated from the old hurts that she went on a long weekend vacation with her mother and had the best time. She is so grateful for the new relationship with her mom.

Another woman, after reading the article in the *New York Times*, told me that she went to her mom's house, unannounced. Once there, she told her mom that she forgave her for abandoning her at a young age. This led to their reconciliation, and her brother and sister were reconciled as well.

Another woman told me about her granddaughter who died of a drug overdose. The grandmother was very bitter and angry with the drug dealer who had sold her granddaughter the drugs. After hearing our story, she realized how bitterness was ruining her life. She prayed for God's help in letting go and eventually was able to forgive the drug dealer. In her case it was not in person. But once she forgave him, she was released from the bitterness and anger that had previously eaten her up.

In the fall of 2011, we attended a prayer breakfast at the

sheriff's office. One of the sheriff's deputies told us about how his partner had been shot and died in his arms. He told us how he had to tell the widow and how his partner's death affected him so much that he left South Florida to come to North Florida. His lack of forgiveness and hatred for the shooter caused him to suffer greatly—physically as well as emotionally. When he heard our story, he told us he felt compelled to drive to the death row prison to see the man who had shot and killed his partner. I don't know if he ever made that trip or not, but the seed was planted in his heart.

I love the stories of forgiveness that I hear, because they all point to the wonderful diversity in what people experience when they choose to forgive. It just looks different for everyone. Here are some things we've learned about forgiveness since we were forced into what many have called the "radical forgiveness" of Conor.

1. *Forgiveness isn't a onetime event.* Peter asked Jesus, "Lord, how many times shall I forgive my brother or sister who sins against me? Up to seven times?" Jesus answered, "I tell you, not seven times, but seventy-seven times" (Matt. 18:21–22). Some translations say "seventy *times* seven," meaning 490 times. But after our experience with Conor, I wonder if that scripture doesn't more accurately refer to the constant and repetitive forgiveness we must give for the same offense.

When I tell the story of forgiving Conor within the week of the shooting, some people recoil. "That's not real forgiveness," they say. "That's an instinct. Real forgiveness takes time." In a way this is true. I forgave Conor, however, when he was in the Leon County jail; but I also might need to forgive him when I walk by Ann's room or when I set the table for Thanksgiving without Ann's dinner plate. Forgiveness is a process, a habit, and a way of life . . . not a distinct act.

2. *Forgiveness isn't primarily a feeling or a sentiment.* Some people believe they are not the types of people who can easily forgive. They look at Andy and me as if we're saints—pious people who speak Scripture to each other in encouragement instead of those who have been known to fight in the cereal aisle over Honey Nut Cheerios. Forgiveness is not the first instinct, nor is it an easy path. It's a decision that says you believe the Bible when it says that vengeance belongs to God.

"Forgiveness must be granted before it can be felt, but it does come eventually," Tim Keller wrote in *The Reason for God*. "It leads to a new peace, a resurrection. It is the only way to stop the spread of the evil."[3] In the hospital, when I asked myself what Ann would want from this, the answer would always come back: "Peace." Andy says it this way: "Because we forgave, we didn't have to go to prison with Conor." Forgiveness brought us a measure of peace that we could not have had otherwise.

3. *Forgiveness has less to do with the person who harmed you than you think.* Mother Teresa is frequently attributed with saying,

> *People are often unreasonable, illogical and self-centered;*
> *Forgive them anyway.*
>
> *If you are kind, people may accuse you of selfish, ulterior motives;*
> *Be kind anyway. . . .*
>
> *If you are honest and frank, people may cheat you;*
> *Be honest and frank anyway. . . .*
>
> *If you find serenity and happiness, they may be jealous;*
> *Be happy anyway.*

The good you do today, people will often forget tomorrow;
Do good anyway.

Give the world the best you have, and it may never be enough;
Give the world the best you've got anyway.

You see, in the final analysis, it is between you and God;
It was never between you and them anyway.[4]

That last line contains much truth. When we forgave Conor, it had more to do with the relationship Andy and I had with Christ rather than the relationship we had with Conor.

4. *Forgiveness doesn't require ignoring the offense.* Forgiveness does not require a willful blindness to other people's failures or misdeeds. It requires truth—an honest evaluation of what's been done and what's been lost—and a determined decision to forgive in spite of that loss. In some translations the Lord's Prayer says, "Forgive us our debts, as we also have forgiven our debtors" (Matt. 6:12). I have prayed with people who are having trouble forgiving, and I try to explain it in a practical way: What does the person owe you? Love? Respect? A nonchaotic childhood? That is their debt against you. Can you forgive that debt? Release it to God for him to collect.

5. *Forgiveness isn't a pardon.* When we decided to forgive Conor, it didn't mean he was less guilty of shooting that gun. It simply meant that we were entrusting his soul and his judgment to God. Conor said that our forgiveness allowed him to accept the responsibility for what he'd done without being condemned. When we refused to be his enemy, we refused to give him the refuge of our hatred—where he could wallow and become, in a way, *our* victim.

Forgiveness allows him to deal with what he'd done. It doesn't mean the injustice should stand or that what he did was okay. It means we don't have to nurse our bitterness and plan ways to get back at the person who hurt us. Instead, we can trust that God, who sits on the throne, is in control of our souls.

6. *Forgiveness does not always mean reconciliation.* Forgiveness is only one side of the coin. The other is repentance. When Andy and I attended a marriage workshop, one of the talks posited that there are two parts to reconciliation. The first is to forgive and forget. Of course, people are not able to forget serious offenses, nor would they want to. Certainly we could never forget that Ann has died. Instead, it means not holding the offense against the other person. In the marriage workshop, we learned not to bring up past hurts if they have already been forgiven.

The other side of the coin? Repent and repair. For reconciliation to occur, the offenders must be sorry for what they have done. They must also be willing to make amends for whatever hurt they caused. Of course, reconciliation is not possible if the offender is not sorry; but forgiveness still is. Forgiveness can exist without re-establishing a relationship and without having a relationship with the offender at all. Furthermore, forgiveness is not saying, "Yes, you may hurt me again."

7. *Forgiveness isn't optional.* One of the most frequent comments we hear goes something like this: "I could never forgive someone if they did that to my family." Others say that our forgiveness is "radical" or "supernatural." Nothing could be further from the truth. We didn't forgive Conor because we're some sort of super-Christians. Rather, forgiveness is a basic Christian requirement. When Jesus tells us to love our enemies, it is not an empty Hallmark-card sentiment. Why does he ask us to forgive? He elaborates, "For if

you forgive other people when they sin against you, your heavenly Father will also forgive you. But if you do not forgive others their sins, your Father will not forgive your sins" (Matt. 6:14–15). This—along with the parable of the unforgiving servant and the teachings of Paul—indicates that we can't withhold forgiveness and expect to receive it.

⌗

One sunny day, Andy and I were walking along the Miccosukee Canopy Road Greenway and stopped at a bench that was donated by the McBrides to honor the memory of our daughter. The bench is placed right along the pathway, so cyclists needing a break, walkers needing a seat, or joggers needing a snack can have a place of rest.

Andy and I sat down on the bench and enjoyed the feel of the sun on our skin. I looked out over the field and remembered the days when Ann would ride her horse BJ to the park on lazy afternoons. As comforting as those memories were, however, I also imagined what might have been. I imagined what Ann's wildlife refuge would have been like . . . Rescued horses would've been munching lazily on the grass while birds of prey flew overhead.

We keep Ann's legacy alive through our work with St. Francis Wildlife Association—work that Conor will someday take up on Ann's behalf. But her story—our story—is about more than a refuge for animals. Rather, this story presents a fuller picture of forgiveness in the ordinary, day-to-day lives of rather typical people.

Forgiveness is not a pardon. But it is a refuge: a place where broken people can come for healing, where the guilty can come for relief, where the wronged can come for hope.

We must develop and maintain the capacity to forgive. He who is devoid of the power to forgive is devoid of the power to love. There is some good in the worst of us and some evil in the best of us. When we discover this, we are less prone to hate our enemies.

—MARTIN LUTHER KING JR.[1]

Q & A WITH CONOR MCBRIDE

Nancy French
Wakulla Correctional Institution
March 2015
(Responses edited and arranged for grammar and clarity)

How did you meet Ann?

Our sophomore year in high school, we were in the same chemistry class . . . But we did not like each other at all. Honestly, I was a judgmental know-it-all. It was an early morning class, so Ann came in tired, grumpy, and unhappy, wearing a hoodie. I thought she and her friend were slackers who didn't care about school, so I didn't want anything to do with them.

The next year, we were in the same English class and sat across from each other in connected, prefab desks. I have clonus, a mild form of cerebral palsy, so I don't have the greatest motor control in my legs. I kept kicking her under the table, but didn't realize it. In my mind, I was just moving my feet.

"What?" she asked, after being kicked one too many times. "What?!"

So, that's how our relationship began.

We really connected later in drama. She was the stage manager for *12 Angry Men*, and I was one of the minor jurors . . . Juror #2. Eventually, we became good friends. We'd hang out and talk for hours. We got along very well, and—eventually—it became romantic. We were best friends, who later fell in love.

Did you and Ann ever talk about faith?

Because of my own personal prejudice against God, we didn't. We started a class together—the Catholic introduction to the faith program, which explained everything it meant to be Catholic. I just wasn't into it. I was only doing it for her, because she was interested in it. I felt like I should probably be involved in faith, but I didn't really understand it.

I remember driving home one night, and I said, "I just don't get it. I don't see the point. What is this? Some people just need that good moral foundation and that guide. But beyond that?"

So, we never talked more about it.

I wish we had.

Please describe your faith journey.

If you had talked to me before all of this, I would've laughed at the idea of God. I didn't believe in him in any way, shape, or form. I was an atheist, because I believed there was no God, that anyone who believed in God was either stupid or deluded, and that most religious individuals were snake oil salesmen. It was all a con.

But when I started dating Ann, I went to mass with her. Interestingly enough, I felt empty as I sat there at Good Shepherd Catholic Church . . . it was a weird emptiness that I couldn't explain. Now I realize that it was God trying to tell me that I was missing something.

When I killed Ann, the whole process of faith started. I had never really prayed before until I was in jail. My first prayers were, "God, help me. I have no idea what's going on." I mean, I knew what I did, but I was confused by it.

I shot her on Sunday. When Kate came to see me, we were both crying. Obviously it was very emotional.

"Conor, no matter what happens," she said, "we love you and forgive you." That was the birthplace of my faith, because normal people don't do that. The human, worldly response to someone killing someone's daughter is to hate that person.

The Grosmaires should've hated me; they should've condemned me. That's the normal reaction. Yet they responded in love and have continued to do that. They've visited, they've written, and I call them every Monday. It's really a tangible forgiveness.

For me, that was proof of God. [Their forgiveness] had to be the love of God shining through them. There's no other explanation for it. It's not normal, and it's not rational. That was the point where I started to believe.

Since then, I've had ups and downs. I didn't know what I was missing. I didn't realize God was there. Now, nothing can change my mind of that. I absolutely, positively know God. There's no doubt in my mind [of his existence]. Andy talked about the love of God, and how God can forgive anything. That's real to me. I've seen that in the Grosmaires. I have friends [in prison] who struggle to believe in forgiveness. They ask, "How can God forgive me?" Yet I've been blessed with this clear sign that it can happen. I guess I needed that . . . some sort of physical proof. It's one thing to say, "God is real." But it's another to show that the love, grace, and forgiveness of God is real too.

I don't know if I would've believed in God without this incident. I'm not saying it was a good thing that this tragedy happened or that it should've happened.

But *because* it happened, I now believe.

Was there a moment of salvation that you remember?

My salvation was a gradual thing. Some people talk about the day they prayed the sinner's prayer—that absolute moment. Looking back, I know Kate and Andy's decision to forgive was that moment for me, but it was more of a gradual realization. A few months after their forgiveness, I began to understand the spiritual impact.

When I was reading about God's forgiveness and God's grace in the Bible, a light went off. "Oh! I know what the Bible is talking about."

Why did you put down Kate's name on your visitation list after you were arrested?

In retrospect, it was of God.

At the time, I didn't know why I put her name down. I knew I didn't put Andy's name down because I was terrified of seeing him. I didn't expect Kate to come. I wasn't expecting her visit at all on that day.

When my name was called at Leon County jail, I walked up to the visitation booth, which is in the middle of a big V. I came out of my cell and—for about thirty feet—I could see her in the window through the plexiglass. My heart was absolutely pounding. All I could think to say is, "I'm so sorry. So, so sorry." Sorry doesn't even begin to encompass the emotion, but I just felt so terrible. Seeing her and facing her was really rough. I wasn't sure what to expect; I just knew I was scared. There was a part of me that really wanted to talk to her. I had a desire to confess, a desire to express how sorry I was and how much I regretted everything. There was a lot of fear and a lot of sorrow to see Kate, whom I knew I'd hurt and was grieving. Yet, she came to see me. [Pause.] I can't really explain it more than that. I can't do it justice with words. I'm sorry.

How frequently do you think of Ann?

I used to be haunted by what I'd done and didn't know how to deal with it.

"How do I get over this?" I asked Sujatha. "I just feel so terrible for what I've done, and I can't stop beating myself up over this."

"Conor, it's never going to be okay," she said. "But you'll come to a place where you'll be okay with it not being okay."

That was the key for me. I'm not okay with the fact that I've killed Ann. But I'm okay with the fact that killing Ann will never be okay. I did a horrible, terrible thing, but I cannot let that hold me down. I need to move forward and be productive, because I really feel a responsibility to live for two lives. I was living for myself before, and that didn't work out too well. I want to live for Ann in the sense of genuinely caring for the things she cared for and doing more than just what I would've done otherwise. Ann was always interested in opening a rehabilitation center for injured raptors, birds of prey. She had a general concern and care about animals, so I wanted to do something in that vein . . . possibly working for St. Francis Wildlife. That's what she would've wanted.

There are some days I look back at what I've done, and it's really rough. I hate myself for it. I'm down on myself. I realize that's not what Ann would've wanted. She'd want me to be productive and to actually live.

Sometimes, I find myself in a place where I remember the good things. Other days, I just remember the bad things. It's always keeping it in context. There was good; there was bad. There's a lot to be learned from it all. I'm not stuck on her death. I don't define her by her death. I don't define myself by killing her.

How do you define yourself?

One of the classes we have here in prison requires you to make a tombstone that has your epitaph. The idea is that you make goals and plans in life to make that epitaph come true in death. On my tombstone, I wrote one word: "forgiven."

Only in forgiveness can I move forward and live, without being trapped by the horrible decision I made. I'm not chained by my past or by beating myself up forever. I'm moving forward, I've forgiven others, because of the forgiveness shown me.

I don't deserve forgiveness at all. But the Grosmaires still chose—out of love—to forgive me.

That's all I need my tombstone to say: forgiven.

Now, it's up to me to live that way.

At the restorative justice circle, were you tempted to obscure things, to tell half-truths, or to lie about that day?

Yes and no. The reason I say that? There was a certain element of fear. I heard a little voice, saying, "Don't tell them."

Thankfully, Sujatha had coached me.

"You have to be completely honest. That's what this is about," she said. "This isn't about making yourself look good, hiding something, or convincing them to give you a lesser sentence. It's about healing, open dialogue, and communication."

There was no room for lying, hiding, or obscuring. It was the hardest thing I've ever done. I was about five feet from Andy. There was nothing between us. Andy and Mrs. Grosmaire were sitting there, and I had to tell them how I killed their daughter, the events of that day, what led up to it, what was going through my head. It would've been an even greater injustice had I lied.

I had to be honest with them. It was the least I could do . . . The only real way I could give back a little of what I'd taken.

What was the one question during the circle that you were most apprehensive to answer?

[On the day of the shooting] I'd left the room and gotten the gun. When I came back, Ann was on the floor, on her knees. That's when I shot her.

Andy asked me this: "So you're telling me you shot her while she was on her knees?"

Confessing to Andy that it happened this way was probably the hardest question to answer.

No, it was definitely the hardest question to answer.

Were you nervous the Grosmaires would take back their forgiveness after the restorative justice circle?

When they shared what it meant to lose their daughter, it gave me such a greater understanding of the loss. I'd already understood it from my perspective, but I didn't even have an inkling of what they were going through. I still don't fully understand. I've never been a parent. I can't know.

But they described the loss, the sorrow, and how much of a waste it seemed to them. They talked about the dirty diapers, the food, helping her with her homework . . . it just made it clear. It opened my eyes to the impact of what I'd done. It was no longer just what I had lost or what I had experienced; it showed me what they were living through.

They shared first; then I shared. Then Sujatha turned it back to them.

"How do you respond to Conor?" she asked them.

That was that moment of [*gasp of breath*] when Sujatha asked that question. I wondered how they would respond after hearing the details of the shooting. I didn't know if they would continue to forgive me, or if they'd say, "You know what? Yeah, this was a bad idea from the beginning. You're sick. You're twisted. We have every right to hate you."

I didn't know what was going to happen, but that's when they told me they'd decided to continue to forgive me.

Do you have friends in prison?

I have a small group of people I associate with and hang out with. You can't say that you can really have friends in prison, because of the environment. But these are people who sit down and read the Bible together. One might say, "I have trouble believing in God, because my relationship with my dad was so bad. I don't understand God, because my dad was abusive." He has trouble understanding a loving God. Everyone has experiences, and we all share and try to encourage one another.

What is your faith practice like now?

Normally, the dormitory I'm in is quiet in the morning, so I try to read my Bible while it's peaceful and not many people are moving around. I try to do it daily, but I'm not great at it. There are also classes that the institution offers. I'm in one now called, "All of Grace," based on a sermon by Charles Spurgeon. We have several Bible studies within the dorm itself. Then my group of friends meets on Thursday. Apart from that, on Sunday afternoons, they have Catholic services. Father Mike comes in and volunteers his time for mass or a communion service. What's really interesting is that the group that meets for mass feels like family. It's a very tight-knit, very loving and caring group. We look out for each other in prison. Frequently, I see people from mass who say, "Hey, how are you doing? I haven't seen you in a while." It's pretty cool. It feels like you step away from prison. It feels like a very secure and comforting place.

Do you fear you'll kill someone again?

I don't know. I don't think any person knows how they will react in any given situation. I know some of the causes and triggers . . . not that there was any one thing. But little factors added up to me exploding. Now, knowing those things, I can address those issues—whether it's my issues with anger, relationship issues, stress from work and school. Those things can be evaluated. Now I'm at a place where I can better address my anger. "Okay," I can ask myself. "Am I all right? Am I doing things that are pushing me to the edge of anger, when I'm going to snap in my everyday life?" I'm not necessarily talking about killing someone, but in my general day to day life. I have to be aware and cognizant of my threshold, my anger, and what triggers it. That's where I am now. I will never do that again. I will never harm someone again, because I am actively making sure I don't.

What do you do to address your anger?

A couple of things. One is spiritual counseling. Scripture, like James 1:19–20, helps. Although I'm not an alcoholic, I'm involved in Alcoholics Anonymous. Some of the principles taught in that class are interesting, like not building up resentment, letting things go, knowing what you can control and what you can't. Most of the things we worry about are completely beyond our control, so there's no reason to get upset about those. Prison has taught me not to worry about people because you can't control them. You can only do what you can. It's helped me to take a step back and realize, "Okay, I'm stressing over things I don't need to stress about."

You've been in prison five years. What is the difference between how you would feel at this moment with the knowledge that you'll get out when you are thirty-nine versus how you'd feel if you had life imprisonment?

I can't even imagine.

I'd have to come to peace with life in prison, and I think I could . . . eventually. But I can't say where I'd be right at this moment. I knew when I was sitting in jail, facing the death penalty and life in prison, I knew I deserved that. I don't deserve a lighter sentence. I killed Ann.

I was only blessed with a lighter sentence because of forgiveness and mercy. It's real and tangible. There is no comparing that pending freedom. I cannot imagine not having a date to look forward to. I know some guys who have life sentences, and they're doing really well. They're productive, they're helping others, they're even teaching classes. But I don't know how long it would've taken me to come to a good place, where I might realize I could do something productive, even if I had to spend my life in prison.

How frequently do you think about getting out of prison?

At least once a day there's a fleeting thought about life after prison, like, *It'll be nice to have a cheeseburger*. While I think about what life will be like, there are a lot of doubts. Kate and Andy have mentioned me getting out, having a life, having a family, having kids. Part of me doubts that working.

I know I still have work to do; I'm still trying to get my mind right. I'm still trying to make sure that my triggers and issues are addressed. I don't know what it's going to be like when I get out.

Do you let yourself imagine a family?

It's something I want. I really wanted kids. I wanted to be a dad. I was really looking forward to that. But the reality is that I made some extremely bad decisions that severely hampered—if not ruined that chance.

What was your biggest regret?

My biggest regret was pulling that trigger and killing Ann.

I know it could've all been avoided, but I never reached out for help.

Do you think the Grosmaires' forgiveness of you is "real"?

It's not "forgiveness for publicity." It's the real thing. They still talk to me; they still tell me they love me. It's a very real thing . . . five years later.

How do you feel about becoming more well-known because this story is now a book?

I don't define myself by my crime. So, okay, a bunch of people will hear this story and might say, "Oh, you're a horrible person."

No, I screwed up. I messed up big time. But that's not the point.

What is the point?

You've heard the story of how two parents forgave the murderer of their daughter.

What can you do in your life?

Who can you forgive?

ACKNOWLEDGMENTS

God gave us the seeds and so many people helped to tend the plant. Thank you to the following individuals who without their contributions and support this book would not have been written:

My friends who encouraged me to write this book—if I named one, I would have to name one hundred. The love and support of our community provided the perfect soil for the seeds to grow.

Chris Park, my literary agent, and garden architect who knew just how the planting should go and provided endless encouragement through the entire growing season.

Nancy French, who worked side by side with me, teaching me, adding the nutrients that made the plant so much fuller than I could have made it on my own.

The editing and design team at Thomas Nelson Publishers, master gardeners who weeded and trimmed until everything looked perfect.

Webster Younce and Thomas Nelson Publishers—I am forever grateful they had faith that my story was worth telling.

Finally, my husband, Andy, who still tends the garden with me.

NOTES

CHAPTER 11

1. Florida Department of Corrections, "10–20–Life, New Mandatory Minimum Prison Sentences," http://www.dc.state.fl.us/secretary/press/1999/1020life.html.

CHAPTER 18

1. "Grosmaire, McBride Families Discuss Healing After Tragedy," *Tallahassee.com*, August 27, 2011, http://archive .tallahassee.com/article/20110829/NEWS01/308290007/ Grosmaire-McBride-families-discuss-healing-after-tragedy.

CHAPTER 19

1. Adam Liptak, "U.S. Prison Population Dwarfs That of Other Nations," *New York Times*, April 23, 2008, http://nytimes .com/2008/04/23/world/americas/23iht-23prison.12253738. html?pagewanted=all&_r=0.
2. Emily Badger, "The Meteoric, Costly and Unprecedented Rise of Incarceration in America," *Washington Post*, April 30, 2014, http:// www.washingtonpost.com/blogs/wonkblog/wp/2014/04/30/ the-meteoric-costly-and-unprecedented-rise-of-incarceration-in -america/.
3. C. S. Lewis, *The Weight of Glory* (New York: HarperCollins, 1976), 46.

CHAPTER 20

1. Paul Tullis, Twitter post, January 12, 2012, http://twitter.com/ptullis.
2. David Belden, "Radical Compassion: Restorative Justice Program Meets Needs of Both Victims," Alternet, January 20, 2013, http://www.alternet.org/radical-compassion-restorative-justice-program-meets-needs-both-victims-and-perpetrators.
3. Timothy Keller, *The Reason for God: Belief in an Age of Skepticism* (New York: Penguin, 2008), 189.
4. Quoted in David Matthew Brown, "*Anyway* Poem by Mother Teresa," *Patheos.com*, July 31, 2012, http://www.patheos.com/blogs/wrestlingwithyourself/2012/07/anyway-poem-by-mother-teresa/.

CLOSING EPIGRAPH

1. Martin Luther King Jr., *The Words of Martin Luther King, Jr.: Second Edition* (Nashville: Thomas Nelson, 2008), 23.

ABOUT THE AUTHORS

Kate Grosmaire became an educator about Restorative Justice after her daughter was killed. She and her husband are the cofounders of the Ann Grosmaire "Be The Change" Fund, a charitable fund to promote forgiveness and restorative justice practices. Kate lives in Tallahassee, Florida.

✦

Nancy French is a three-time *New York Times* bestselling author who has written books with former Alaska Governor Sarah Palin, Chinese dissident Bob Fu, Iraq war vet and Constitutional lawyer David French, Olympic gold medalist Shawn Johnson, and Bristol Palin. Read about these—and other books—at www.NancyFrench.com and connect with her on Twitter at @NancyAFrench.